independent clauses together
conjunction+comma holds them together

For
And
Nor
But
Or
Yet
So

Stylebook

A USAGE GUIDE FOR WRITERS AND EDITORS

EDITED BY ROBERT O. GROVER

NINTH EDITION

Copyright 2001, 1997, 1994, 1990, 1984, 1981, 1977
by U.S.News & World Report LP
1050 Thomas Jefferson Street NW, Washington, DC 20007-3837
Ninth Edition, revised 2001

Design by Michele Chu.

This book was composed by Janie S. Price. Printed in the United States of America.

Library of Congress Cataloging-in-Publication Data
U.S.News & World Report Stylebook: a usage guide for writers and editors
Edited by Robert O. Grover—9th ed.
    p. cm.
    Rev. ed. of: U.S.news & world report stylebook for writers and editors/
        Robert O. Grover. 8th ed. 1997
    ISBN 1-931469-10-5
    1. Journalism—Style manuals. 2. Journalism—Terminology. I. Grover, Robert O., 1942– .
II. U.S.news & world report lp. III. Title: U.S.news & world report stylebook: a usage guide for writers and editors
PN4783.R6 2001
808'.027—dc21   2001001693

INTRODUCTION

The *U.S.News & World Report Stylebook: A Usage Guide for Writers and Editors* is designed primarily to quickly and easily answer staffers' questions about style and usage, but it is also useful for anyone seeking guidelines to clear writing.

Most of the entries provide cold, dry, practical answers to such value-free questions as whether certain numbers should be rendered in words or in figures. Other entries go to the heart and soul of a publication, encompassing everything from how to deal with quotations that include vulgarity and obscenity to how to handle language that reflects gender, racial, ethnic, or religious bias.

The stylebook is mostly nuts and bolts, of primary day-to-day interest to desk editors and proofreaders, but because it also helps set the tone for the magazine, it should be read by writers, editors, photographers, researchers, fact checkers, librarians, designers, and illustrators alike.

A portion of any profits from sales of the stylebook will be used to support adult-literacy programs.

Your comments and suggestions are welcome. Please send them to *rgrover@usnews.com* or News Desk Chief, *U.S.News & World Report,* 1050 Thomas Jefferson Street NW, Washington, DC 20007-3837.

ACKNOWLEDGMENTS

I am indebted to the scores of people whose suggestions, support, and gentle criticism helped shape this book and continue to keep it accurate, useful, and up to date. Special thanks to the members of the stylebook committee: Liz Brooke, Jim Bock, Judy Shapleigh, Susan Vavrick, John Sellers, and Ben Wildavsky; to Steve Smith, Karen Chevalier, Peter Cary, and Anastasia Tasoulis, who provided invaluable resources and support; to Michele Chu, whose design skills made the book a pleasure to look at and easy to read; to Janie Price, who tirelessly composed the typography; to Richard Thompson, whose wit and artistry make reading the book such good fun, and to the many editors, writers, fact checkers, researchers, proofreaders, librarians, artists, news assistants, media colleagues, friends, students, and readers of the magazine whose influence and ideas did so much to make this book useful and this project a pleasure. They include, but are by no means limited to: Ed Albaugh, Kent Allen, Terry Atlas, Bruce Auster, Dixie Barlow, Michael Barone, Paul Bedard, Gloria Borger, Mary Brophy Marcus, Lori Buckner, Judy Burke, Julie Burrow, Tim Byers, Ken Campbell, Kathy Coates, Chanté Cobb, Avery Comarow, Julie Corwin, Susan Dentzer, Tom Dienes, Brian Duffy, Zakiya Dunmore, Shirley Dutchak, Lynne Edwards, Scott Ellsworth, Eric Erickson, Jim Fallows, Charlie Fenyvesi, Mike Fingerhuth, Josh Fischman, Kathleen Flynn, Kate Forsyth, Myke Freeman, Joe Galloway, Dan Garcia, Don Gatling, Thom Geier, Ted Gest, Carla Giammichele, Norm Goldstein, MaryAnne Golon, David Griffin, Elizabeth Gross, Dorothy Grover, Avi Gupta, Wray Herbert, Katia Hetter, Kenneth Hooton, Mary Jean Hopkins, Maggie Hume, Diane Javaid, Nelea Johnson, Judy Katzung, Michal Keeley, Robin Knight, Susan Lawrence, Susan LeClair, Virginia Lee, Jeff Lehman, Cindy Leitner, Lucy Leitner, Joyce Littlejohn, Lew Lord, Mary Lord, Jeff MacMillan, Ric Manhard, Mimi McLoughlin, Mary Lu Meixell, Peter Meredith, Rick Newman, Kim Payne, Cindy Phelps, Penny Pickett, John Plunkett, Doug Podolsky, Erika Pontarelli, Victoria Pope, Mary Beth Protomastro, Chitra Ragavan, Lee Rainie, Erin Randall, Sueyen Rhee, Susan Riker, Lesley Rogers, Sheryl Rosenthal, Mike Ruby, Nicole Schofer, Mark Schulte, Jennifer Seter, Howard Sewell, Joe Shapiro, Jeffery Sheler, Betsy Sherman, George Shevlin, Allan Siegal, Roger Simon, John Simons, Sara Sklaroff, Cathy Sweeney, Cheri Temoney, Susie Thomas, Mark Titus, Jay Tolson, Jeff Trimble, Kathy Trimble, John Walcott, Deborah Wallis, Ken Walsh, Alan Weinstein, Len Wiener, Tim Zimmermann, and the Journalism 202 students at the University of Maryland's Philip Merrill College of Journalism.

Robert O. Grover

Entry titles are alphabetized. For many questions, you can go right to the word or phrase you are seeking. **Connecticuter,** for example, stands without elaboration, meaning that the usage is acceptable as written. For other questions, you might need to go to a general category. If you want to know, say, how to handle titles of cabinet officers, consult the **titles of persons** entry. If you want to know what residents of Djibouti are called, you can find it in the **nations and regions** table.

Examples are in red type (Do it this way, if you please). Examples that should be set italic, such as book titles, are in red italic type (*The Firm*). Subheadings and cross-references are in small caps (EXCEPTIONS; See FAIRNESS). The electronic "names" and "places" files, which list people, organizations, and geographic names in the news, are available in the *U.S. News* computer system, as is the stylebook itself.

When a usage is proscribed, do not use it unless an exception has been agreed upon by top editors and the style editor. When an entry says a usage should be "avoided," don't use it unless you have exhausted alternatives. When several options are listed, use whichever one best suits the matter at hand.

For questions not explicitly addressed in this book, use analogy and, should that fail, use common sense in consultation with the style editor.

The electronic stylebook

Anyone with access to the *U.S. News* TeamBase system can call up the electronic version of the *U.S. News* stylebook. Many editors rely exclusively on the electronic stylebook, which has the advantage of containing all new entries and the latest updates. Get the electronic stylebook by going to the stylebook-usn queue and calling up the "style" file in "read" mode. To find a word, hit ctrl/f and type the word you seek in the dialog box.

To check the list of names in the news, call up the "names" file in stylebook-usn. To check names of places, call up the "places" file.

If you have questions or problems, please consult any desk editor for assistance (Ext. 2568).

When a style change is made, it will appear immediately in the electronic stylebook. A note about major changes will be sent to all staffers via Eudora.

ages and eras

A

a, an. Before a sounded *h,* use *a;* before a silent *h* and vowel sounds, use *an:* a historic, an herb, an eye, an *m* (sounds as if it begins with an *e*), but a *u* (sounds as if it begins with *y*).

abbreviations. Used judiciously, abbreviations save space and help speed the reader along. When overused, however, they can hinder comprehension and clutter type. Some abbreviations, such as TNT, DDT, FBI, AFL-CIO, and FM, are better known than the words they stand for, and when the context makes their meaning clear they can be used without explanation on all references. Some others that are generally familiar, like GDP, can be used on first reference in a tight lead but should be spelled out as soon as possible in a story. In most cases, the full name of an agency, organization, or company should be used on first reference. Exceptions are noted under individual entries. If an abbreviation is unfamiliar, its first use should appear close to the spelled-out name so the reader can make the connection. Put an abbreviation in parentheses directly after the words it stands for only when a later appearance of the abbreviation would otherwise be unclear. For capitalization and punctuation, which often vary from one abbreviation to another, consult the entries below as well as entries for particular abbreviations in this book and in dictionaries. See ACRONYMS, ADDRESSES, AMPERSAND, APOSTROPHE, CHARTS AND TABLES, COLLEGES AND UNIVERSITIES, COMPANY NAMES, COMPASS DIRECTIONS, INITIALS, METRIC SYSTEM, MILITARY TITLES, MONTHS, NATIONS AND REGIONS, PLURALS, SMALL CAPS, STATES, TIME, WEIGHTS AND MEASURES, and the electronic NAMES and PLACES lists.

ABCs

ABM. Acceptable on second reference to *antiballistic missile.* ABM treaty.

abortion-debate terminology. Acceptable terms include antiabortion activists, abortion opponents, abortion-rights activists, and pro-abortion rights. Except when we are quoting someone, avoid using *pro-life, right-to-life, pro-choice,* and *anti-choice,* which are at worst imprecise and at best politically loaded. Don't use *pro-abortion* unless it accurately describes the person's or group's position. Don't use *pro-lifers* or *pro-choicers* except in quoted matter and then only when essential.

INFANTICIDE is the killing of an infant, so we should not use it in references to abortion.

FETICIDE is the illegal killing of a fetus, so we should not use it references to abortion unless the abortion under discussion is forbidden by law. If a government, for example, forbade abortion that was performed solely for the purpose of sex selection, such an abortion would correctly be called feticide.

PARTIAL-BIRTH ABORTION is used in legislative language, but the term is arguably inflammatory, so if you must use it, put "partial-birth" in quotation marks. Alternative terms, which have problems of their own, include "a form of late-term abortion" (which is so broad that it is obfuscating) and "intact dilation and extraction" (which is obfuscatingly clinical).

PRE-BORN BABY is a logical impossibility. Use it only when quoting someone.

aboveground (adjective)

above-water (adjective)

academic degrees. See BACHELOR OF ARTS DEGREE, DOCTOR OF PHILOSOPHY, etc.

academy. Capitalize in a name; lowercase alone: United States Naval Academy (the Naval Academy, but the academy, a naval academy), the French Academy. See COLLEGES AND UNIVERSITIES.

accent marks. See DIACRITICS.

accents. Do not misspell or put quotation marks around words that you regard as peculiarities of speech without a compelling reason. The primary implication is derogatory, and, besides, the trouble might be in your ear. See QUOTATIONS.

accords. Capitalize in an official name; lowercase alone: Camp David Accords, Dayton Peace Accords, but Dayton accords, the accords, Oslo accords (not the official name).

Achilles heel. Achilles tendon, but in literal references, use 's: "The head of the arrow for Achilles's heel smiled in its sleep."

acquired immune deficiency syndrome. AIDS is acceptable on all references if the context makes the meaning clear.

acronyms are pronounceable words formed from the first letter or letters of a series of words: HUD for Department of Housing and Urban Development; LANTIRN for low-altitude navigation and targeting infrared (system) for night. Some acronyms, through long-standing usage, are spelled caps and lowercase or all lowercase: Tass, Hamas, Rand, snafu, radar. Check individual entries in this book, the electronic NAMES list, and the dictionaries for guidance. Write acronyms without points. Constructions that are not pronounceable words—AAUW (American Association of University Women), for instance—are initialisms but are not acronyms. Plurals are normally formed by adding an *s*: PAC, PACs. See ABBREVIATIONS and SMALL CAPS.

act. Capitalize when part of a name; lowercase alone: Immigration and Nationality Act (the act), an act of Congress, acts of Congress, Act I (the act).

active voice. In the active voice, the subject does the acting (*He opened the door*); in the passive voice, the subject is acted upon (*The door was opened*). Although there are times when use of the passive is preferred, such as when you don't know or don't want to reveal the doer of the action, those situations are few. In most cases, use the active voice, which is more vigorous, more natural, and usually less wordy.

act of God. As a legal term, it means an occurrence that is due entirely to the forces of nature and could not reasonably have been prevented. In nonlegal references, consider using the term *act of nature* instead.

A.D. Usually precedes the year; no comma: bones dating to A.D. 357.

addresses. Spell out and capitalize Street, Avenue, Alley, Route, etc., including numbered streets below 10 when part of a specific location: Fifth Avenue, Coates Street, but the streets of New York. Abbreviate compass points, using a period when the letter comes in front of the street (6 W. 42nd Street) and no period when the letters come after the street (24th and N streets NW), but spell out the compass points in a street name when there is no address number: Jamal lived on West 42nd Street. Do not put a comma between the state and the ZIP code. When giving a complete address, use Postal Service state abbreviations; otherwise use the traditional abbreviations listed in the STATES entry. In general, distinguish Web site URLs and E-mail addresses by putting them in italics (or in roman when the sentence is italicized), unless the layout calls for some other distinguishing characteristic, such as boldface.

When URLs and E-addresses break over a line, drop any line-breaking hyphens:

Go to *http://www.usnews
.com* for the latest.

Please reply to *rgrover@us
news.com*

ad hoc (adverb and adjective)

adjectives, multiple. Break them up. This sentence may be difficult to understand: *Farmers are planting from fence to fence to meet soaring world food demand.* Better: Farmers are planting from fence to fence to meet the world's soaring demand for food.

adjustable-rate (adjective)

administration. Capitalize in names; lowercase otherwise: Food and Drug Administration, Grant administration, the administration.

admiral. Capitalize before a name; lowercase otherwise. Abbreviate, Adm., before full name; spell out otherwise: Adm. Aaron Aument (Admiral Aument, the admiral). See MILITARY TITLES.

admission(s). In official titles, follow an individual's preference: Dean of Admission Keisha Jordan, but make generic references plural: She wanted to become an admissions director.

adopted, adoptive. Children are adopted; parents are adoptive. Do not identify people that way unless the information is clearly germane to the story. To indicate consanguinity, use terms like birthparent or biological mother rather than *natural parent,* which implies that adoptive parents are unnatural.

adrenaline/Adrenalin. The substance produced by the adrenal gland is lowercase and ends with an *e.* It is also called epinephrine. The trademark for the synthetic or chemically extracted product is capitalized and has no *e* at the end.

Advanced Placement. Capitalize in references to the trademarked classes: the Advanced Placement Program, Advanced Placement English, Advanced Placement geography.

adverb placement. The best placement for an adverb in a compound-verb sentence is usually where it sounds most natural, more often than not between the parts of the compound verb. In some cases, placement has no effect on the meaning of a sentence: They have vociferously argued about finances. They have argued vociferously about finances. In others, placement is crucial to meaning. In the sentence Linda says she frequently finds misplaced gloves, the finding is frequent. In Linda says she finds frequently misplaced gloves, the misplacing is frequent. See ONLY.

adviser

affect/effect. As a verb, affect means to influence or to make a pretense of: How did she affect the outcome? He affected a nonplused attitude. Effect, as a verb, means to bring about a result: The movers effected a speedy transition; as a noun, it means a result: The music had a soothing effect on everyone. Affect is used as a noun in psychology, where it means an emotion attached to an idea, object, etc.

AFL-CIO. American Federation of Labor–Congress of Industrial Organizations. The abbreviation is acceptable on all references. See UNION NAMES.

African-American. See (-)AMERICAN, BLACK, and RACIAL DESIGNATIONS.

after-dinner (adjective)

agency. Capitalize in a name; lowercase alone: Central Intelligence Agency, Agency for International Development, the agency.

ages. Use figures for ages of people and animals: Suzanne was 19 years old; a 5-year-old hamster; a man in his 50s; the police officer, age 27; the boys, ages (not *aged*) 15 to 17; the 4-year-old was hungry. Use figures for inanimate objects 10 and above: the 15-year-old building, the five-year-old plan. See BOY, GIRL, and THIS WEEK.

ages and eras. Capitalize historical designations: Stone Age, Dark Ages, Middle Ages, Jazz Age, Paleozoic Era, Renaissance, Pleistocene Epoch, Pennsylvanian Period, Early Bronze Age, Late Bronze Age. Lowercase terms that are merely descriptive: space age, nuclear age, atomic age, computer age, big-band era, Reagan era. Capitalize Ice Age when referring to the Pleistocene Epoch; lowercase otherwise: Ice Age humans, but the latest ice age. See HISTORIC EVENTS and NEW AGE.

agreement. Capitalize as part of an official name; lowercase standing alone: General Agreement on Tariffs and Trade (the agreement), the U.S.-Mexico trade agreement, the SALT II agreement of 1979.

AIDS (acquired immune deficiency syndrome). Abbreviation is acceptable on all references if the context makes the meaning clear.

aircraft. For details, *Jane's All the World's Aircraft* is helpful. Note some cases in which *U.S. News* style varies from *Jane's.*

U.S.-MADE COMMERCIAL PLANES are usually identified by numbers or letters and numbers. Some planes also are given names, which may be used or omitted as desired. The maker's name also may be used or omitted: Lockheed L-1011 TriStar (L-1011, Lockheed L-1011, TriStar), Boeing 747 (747), McDonnell Douglas DC-10 (DC-10), Air Force One, Maid of the Seas.

U.S. MILITARY PLANES are customarily designated by numbers, with prefixed letters to indicate basic functions: A for attack, B for bomber, C for cargo, F for fighter, S for antisubmarine, T for trainer, etc. Often a letter is added at the end to show an adaptation or order in a series. Names, when they exist, may be used or omitted as desired: F-4D Phantom (F-4D, Phantom), B-52H, C-9B, A-4, F-15A, S-3A, TA-4J.

RUSSIAN PLANES are generally designated by numbers, with prefixes that are abbreviations of the makers' or designers' names: Tu for Tupolev, MiG for Mikoyan & Gurevich, M for Myasishchev, Su for Sukhoi, Yak for Yakovlev, Il for Ilyushin, etc. NATO specialists designate Russian planes with names beginning with F for fighter, B for bomber, C for cargo, H for helicopter, M for miscellaneous fixed-wing planes, etc. These names may be used or omitted as desired: MiG-25 Foxbat (MiG-25, Foxbat), Il-76 Candid, Yak-28 Brewer, Firebar, M-4 Bison, Tu-144 Charger, Tu-26 Backfire, Su-19 Fencer.

airfare

Air Force. Capitalize when referring to a particular country's organization: the U.S. Air Force, an Air Force bomber, the French Air Force (the Air Force), the French and U.S. air forces, an air force.

Air Force One

Air Force Reserve, the Reserve, the Reserves, but reservists when referring to individual members

A

airline, air line, airways. The generic spelling is *airline,* but see individual entries in the electronic NAMES list for variations in company names.

airtime

Alabama (Ala., AL in addresses)

Alabamian

Alaska (AK in addresses; do not abbreviate otherwise)

Alaskan

Alberta. Abbreviate, Alta., only in charts, maps, and tables.

Albertan

Allah. See DEITY and ISLAM.

Alley. Capitalize in an address. See ADDRESSES.

alliance. Capitalize as part of an official name; lowercase in unofficial names and alone: Alliance for Responsible Health Policy (the alliance), Atlantic alliance (not the official name of NATO).

Allies, Allied. Capitalize only in a name or in reference to groupings historically known as the Allies, the nations that opposed Germany in World Wars I and II. Lowercase otherwise, as when applied to partners of the United States or to allies of any nation. Do not capitalize allies or allied when referring to NATO: The Allies defeated the Central Powers in 1918 (the Allies); the Allied debacle at the Somme; the NATO allies (the allies); allies of the United States in NATO; U.S. allies in Europe and Asia.

all out. She goes all out, but an all-out effort.

all right. Everything is all right, but He's an all-right guy.

almanacs, names of. Set italic. See BOOK TITLES and TITLES OF WORKS.

alphabetizing. See COLLEGES AND UNIVERSITIES and INDEXING.

alternate/alternative. As an adjective, alternate means every other: Meetings were held on alternate Sundays. Alternative as a noun means a choice between two or more things: An alternative to the church was the school; as an adjective, it also means pertaining to the unconventional: The dropouts published an alternative newspaper.

a.m. See TIME.

ambassador. Capitalize with a name; lowercase otherwise: Ambassador Marcus Brine (Ambassador Brine), the U.S. ambassador to Switzerland, the ambassador.

amendment. Capitalize in a name; lowercase otherwise: Fifth Amendment, 14th Amendment, the Boland amendment, the amendment, an amendment, Maryland's Equal Rights Amendment (it is in effect), but federal equal rights amendment (it has not been adopted).

(-)American. Hyphenate most foreign-heritage combinations: African-American, Irish-American, Italian-American, Japanese-American, Mexican-American, but Latin American, Hispanic American.

AM/FM-cassette player

ampersand (&). Use for *and* in company and firm names, even when the company prefers to use *and.* Use *and* in names of governmental units; colleges and universities; unions; and trade, nonprofit, and professional groups. Write abbreviations without spaces: R&D, B&B.

animals. Refer to animals as *that* and *which,* unless they are named: He chased the deer, which was fast; She rode Stewball, who was slow.

anointing of the sick. See SACRAMENTS.

another/an additional. *Another* may be used when the amount is the same: They borrowed $500. They borrowed another $500. But when the amount is different, use *an additional* or *more:* They borrowed an additional $200. They borrowed $2,000 more.

Antarctic, Antarctica, the Antarctic, Antarctic Ocean

ante( ). Generally solid except before an *e* or a capitalization or in classical expressions: antediluvian, antemeridian, but ante meridiem (a.m.).

anti( ). Solid except before *i* or a capitalization or in confusing made-up combinations and words hyphenated by the dictionary: antiabortion, antiapartheid, antiaircraft, antiballistic missile, anti-intellectualism, anti-American, anti-bias, anti-union, anti-dumping.

antiballistic missile system

antiballistic missile treaty. ABM treaty is acceptable on second reference.

anti-Christ. An opponent of or disbeliever in Christ.

Antichrist. The biblical antagonist of Christ.

antisemitic describes people who discriminate against or persecute Jews. Do not use in reference to Jews or gentiles who oppose Israeli policies.

anymore (adverb): nowadays, at present; any more: anything additional.

anyplace (adverb): can't go anyplace, **but** in any place, to any place.

anytime or at any time

apostrophe. possessives of singular words are normally formed by adding *'s:* a man's home, James's friend, Los Angeles's weather, Jesus's teachings.

IN A FEW PARTICULAR EXPRESSIONS, especially before the word *sake,* only an apostrophe is used to form the possessive: for goodness' sake, for convenience' sake, for conscience' sake, for righteousness' sake.

POSSESSIVES OF PLURAL WORDS that have become plural by addition of *s* or *es* are formed by an apostrophe only: leaders' views, the Joneses' house, General Motors' parking lot, the United States' point of view.

POSSESSIVES OF ITALICIZED WORDS should be avoided by writing around them. If you must use one, romanize the *'s:* the *Times*'s opinion.

FOR PLURALS OF LETTERS, use *s* when it's clear (GIs, HMOs). Use *'s* when it would be confusing if *s* alone were added (SOS's), with single letters (S's, A's), with lowercase letters used as nouns (x's and y's), and in abbreviations with periods (M.A.'s).

FOR PLURALS OF NUMBERS, add only *s:* F-16s, 1990s, the '30s.

IN PLURALS OF PROPER NAMES, do not use an apostrophe or alter spelling: all the Marys, two Germanys, 1957 Pontiacs, two Tornados.

IN THE NAME OF A COMPANY, association, union, government agency, or military unit, use an apostrophe if the organization's official name does so: National Governors' Association, but Reserve Officers Training Corps, Department of Veterans Affairs.

ATTRIBUTIVE NOUNS. When a noun is used more as an adjective than as a possessive, the apostrophe may be dropped: teachers union, Teamsters hall.

IN GERUND CONSTRUCTIONS (where a verb is used as a noun), use an apostrophe: The Secret Service would not hear of the president's going out alone. A test of this construction: You would not write: "I will not hear of him going out alone." You would write: "I will not hear of his going out alone." If the language becomes confusing or too complicated, consider rewriting.

FOR TRAVEL TIME, use a hyphen construction or an apostrophe construction, but do not mix them: a two-hour flight or a two hours' flight but not *a two-hours' flight.*

JOINT POSSESSION. When ownership is joint, use an apostrophe only with the last owner (Bill and Julie's children); when ownership is individual, use an apostrophe after all owners (Bill's and Julie's wallets). See DOUBLE GENITIVE and PLURALS.

appendix. Capitalize as in Appendix A; lowercase when alone.

April. Do not abbreviate except in charts and tables. See DATES and MONTHS.

Arabic names. Confusion arises over spelling and what parts of a name to use, especially on second reference. Variations have grown out of Western efforts to reproduce Arabic sounds: A French administrator might spell a name with an *-oun* and an American reporter with a *-un* or a *-ur,* depending on the writer's ear and education. Some frequently used Arabic names have acquired generally accepted spellings, and a number of Arabs westernize their names. Follow their preferences. Where neither a personal preference nor an agreed spelling exists, use the system of transliteration devised by the Library of Congress. Ignore the apostrophelike marks and the hyphens before *al.* In most cases, use only the last word of a name in subsequent references.

SAUDI PRINCES are known by their first names: Prince Bandar ibn Abdul-Aziz (Prince Bandar, Bandar).

A

BREAKDOWN. *Gamal Abdel Nasser* was formed as follows: *Gamal* (the individual's name) *Abdel Nasser* (father's name). *Abdel Nasser* comes from *Abd* (worshiper of) *el* (the) *Nasser* (Victorious One—one of the names of God). Sometimes a grandfather's name or a family name is added. Sometimes a particle meaning *son of* or *daughter of* is inserted before the father's name and the grandfather's name: *ibn, bin, ben* (son of); *bint* (daughter of). Spell it *ibn* unless another spelling is firmly established. "The" appears as *al, el, ed, as, ud, ul, ur.* Unless usage or individual preference dictates otherwise, use it only with a full name, spell it *al,* and connect it with a hyphen to the following word.

GENERAL RULES. Follow the spellings in the electronic NAMES list, then in *Webster's New World College Dictionary* and *Webster's Biographical Dictionary.* If the individual has westernized the name, use that spelling, and use the name the individual elects for subsequent mention unless it is too cumbersome. In the absence of a known preference, use the established form and spelling. If there is disagreement about form or spelling, get as close as possible to standard press practice.

HELP WITH QUESTIONS. Ask an Arabic-speaking member of the staff; the Near East Section of the Library of Congress; the Foreign Service Institute of the State Department; country desks of the State Department; and the press officers of Arab diplomatic missions.

arabic numerals. See NUMBERS.

arch( ). Solid except before capitalization: archenemy.

Arctic, the Arctic, Arctic Circle, but lowercase arctic when merely describing very cold conditions.

areas with special and familiar names. See GEOGRAPHIC NAMES, GEOGRAPHIC TERMS, and LOCATIONS.

Arizona (Ariz., AZ in addresses)

Arizonan

Arkansan

Arkansas (Ark., AR in addresses)

Armistice Day is now called Veterans Day.

Army. Capitalize when referring to a specific country's organization and when part of the name of a unit; lowercase generic references and when standing alone in reference to a unit: the U.S. Army (the Regular Army, the all-volunteer Army, the Army), the Russian Army (the Army), the American Army, but America's army, the U.S. and Russian armies, an army, the 7th Army (the army).

Army Reserve, the Reserve, a Reserve major, the Reserves, but reserves and reservists when referring to individual members

Article. Capitalize as in Article III of the Constitution; lowercase alone: the article.

articles, titles of. Use quotation marks. See TITLES OF WORKS.

as great as/greater than. They don't mean the same thing. If Andy makes $50,000 a year and Amy makes $200,000, Amy's salary is four times *as great as* Andy's and three times *greater than* Andy's. The same kind of problem exists with "times more," "times higher," and "times larger." *Times smaller* is mathematically impossible; use a percent or fraction instead.

Asian is generally preferred to *Oriental* for references to people.

assault weapon/assault rifle. These terms are problematic and should only be used advisedly. See FIREARMS.

Assembly. Capitalize when referring to the United Nations General Assembly, to a country's national assembly, or to a state's general assembly: the Indiana General Assembly (the General Assembly, the Assembly), the Oregon Legislative Assembly, the assemblies of Indiana and Kentucky, the French National Assembly (the National Assembly, the Assembly).

associate degree. Wording varies from one institution to another. Some common examples: associate in arts degree (A.A.), associate in science degree (A.S.), associate in applied science degree (A.A.S.), and associate degree in nursing (A.D.N.). If you must use only one word in a tight space: an associate's.

associate justice. Associate justice is the formal title of Supreme Court justices other than the chief justice, but justice is an acceptable alternative. Capitalize before a name; lowercase alone: Associate Justice Sandra Day O'Connor (Justice Sandra Day O'Connor, Justice O'Connor, the associate justice, the justice).

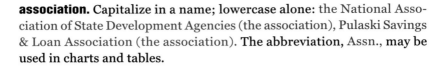

association. Capitalize in a name; lowercase alone: the National Association of State Development Agencies (the association), Pulaski Savings & Loan Association (the association). The abbreviation, Assn., may be used in charts and tables.

assure. To promise confidently. Use *ensure* when meaning to make sure or make safe. Use *insure* with regard to insurance.

asterisks. Put them next to the type to which they refer with no space between: $7,500*, *In 1972 dollars.

at large. Do not hyphenate as a title; hyphenate when used adjectivally: Delegate at Large Stegman, the delegate at large, the delegate-at-large election.

attorney, U.S. Capitalize before a full name; lowercase otherwise: U.S. Attorney Anna Basham (the U.S. attorney).

attorney general, attorneys general. Capitalize before a name; lowercase otherwise. Do not abbreviate: Attorney General Roy Vondy, the attorney general.

audiocassette, audiotape

auger/augur. An auger is a tool. As a noun, augur is a prophet; as a verb, it means to prophesy.

August. See DATES and MONTHS.

auto driver, automaker, auto repairman, autoworker

automatic/semiautomatic weapons. An automatic fires as long as the trigger is held or until the ammunition is exhausted. A semiautomatic fires once and reloads each time the trigger is pulled. See FIREARMS.

automobiles. two-door sedan, a two-door, V-8, the car has six cylinders, a six-cylinder engine.

Avenue. Capitalize when part of an address. Do not abbreviate. See ADDRESSES.

average/mean/median. For nontechnical uses, *average* and *mean* are the same thing: the result of dividing the sum of a group of numerical values by the number of values. The average of 3, 7, and 14 is 8 (24 divided by 3). *Median* is the middle figure in a group of figures arranged by size (the median of 3, 7, and 14 is 7). In situations where extreme values tend to skew the result, *median* might provide a more representative figure than *average* would. For example, in a neighborhood containing an $80,000 house, a $100,000 house, a $120,000 house, a $140,000 house, and a $2 million house, the most expensive house pushes the average (mean) price of a house in the neighborhood to $488,000. The more representative median price (an equal number of houses selling above and below) is $120,000.

AWACS (airborne warning and control system) planes. Boeing E-3A.

awhile. They played awhile, they played for a while, and they took a while are all acceptable, but do not use *awhile* following a preposition (*They played for awhile*).

ax (axes)

big bang

B-1B(s). See AIRCRAFT.

baby boom, baby boom generation, baby boomer

baby-sit (verb), baby sitter (noun), baby-sitting (noun and adjective)

bachelor of arts degree (B.A. or A.B.), bachelor's degree, bachelor's

bachelor of science degree (B.S.), bachelor's degree, bachelor's

backcountry

back door (noun), backdoor (adjective)

backdown (noun), back down (verb)

back fence (noun), back-fence (adjective)

backflash

backflow

backslash

back stairs (noun), backstairs (adjective)

back track (noun), backtrack (verb)

back up (verb), backup (noun and adjective)

backyard (noun and adjective)

backyard, America's. Some find certain uses of this expression objectionable, contending that it implies a patronizing attitude toward neighbors of the United States, so use the term advisedly, if at all.

bacteria. The singular is bacterium. Don't write *a bacteria*. See INFECTIOUS ORGANISMS.

ball. ball three; three balls and two strikes, **but** a 3-2 count

B&B(s). Acceptable on second reference to bed-and-breakfast(s) when the meaning is clear.

Bangladeshi(s). Citizen(s) of Bangladesh. Use Bengali(s) in references to Bengali-speaking residents of Bangladesh and India.

baptism

Baptists. Four major divisions are the Southern Baptist Convention; the National Baptist Convention, U.S.A. Inc.; the National Baptist Convention of America; and the American Baptist Churches in the U.S.A. Refer to Baptist groups by name; it is incorrect to write "the Baptist church" except in reference to a local congregation. Baptist groups do not have bishops, but they have a structure of boards and agencies at various levels. Use of the term "Reverend" is problematic among Baptists. It is best to avoid titles, although members of the Baptist clergy are generally referred to as ministers. A minister who leads a congregation is usually a pastor. Although deacons are ordained to assist pastors and do similar work, they are laypersons, not members of the clergy. The organizational structure of each group is somewhat different, but terminology is similar: Southern Baptist Convention (the convention, the denomination); First Baptist Church (the church); John J. Pomeroy, pastor of the First Baptist Church (the pastor, Pomeroy or John J. Pomeroy, a Baptist minister or clergyman); Lorenzo T. Howard, a deacon in the First Baptist Church (the deacon, Howard).

baron, baronet. See NOBILITY.

baroque. Capitalize when referring to the style of art and architecture that flourished from 1600 to 1750; lowercase in generic references: a Baroque opera, the skateboard's baroque design.

barrel(s). Use abbreviation, bbl., only in charts, maps, and tables.

Bastille Day

battalion. Capitalize when part of a name; lowercase alone: 4th Battalion (the battalion, the battalion commander).

battle cruiser

battlefront

battles. Capitalize when the name is well known: Battle of Britain, Battle of the Bulge, First Battle of Bull Run, but the battles of Bull Run, the battle at Bull Run, the battle.

bay. Capitalize when part of a name; lowercase otherwise: Matagorda Bay (the bay).

BBC. When clear, acceptable on first reference to British Broadcasting Corp.

B.C. Follows year or century; no comma unless year has five or more digits: painted in 2500 B.C., 12,500 B.C.

bear market (noun), bear-market (adjective)

bed-and-breakfast (noun and adjective). B&B is acceptable on second reference when the meaning is clear.

belt. Capitalize in combinations for such recognizable areas as Corn Belt, Cotton Belt, and Sun Belt, but lowercase rust belt (and similar terms) because there is no consensus on its boundaries. See BIBLE BELT.

belt tightening (noun), belt-tightening (adjective)

beltway. Capitalize in names: Capital Beltway, Baltimore Beltway; lowercase alone: cruising the beltway, an inside-the-beltway mentality.

benchmark. A standard in measuring quality or value; bench mark: a surveyor's mark made on a permanent landmark.

bestseller (noun and adjective), bestselling

between/from. Use *and* with *between:* They shoot between 50 and 250 rounds daily. Use *to* with *from:* They shoot from 50 to 250 rounds daily.

bi( ). Combines solid except before a capitalized word or *i.*

biannual/biennial. Biannual (twice a year) is often confused with biennial (once every two years). You can avoid confusion by replacing the former with semiannual.

bias. See EPITHETS, ETHNIC IDENTIFICATION, FAIRNESS, GENDER BIAS, HE/SHE, MAN, and RACIAL DESIGNATIONS.

Bible, the. Capitalize, but lowercase in figurative sense: the volleyballers' bible.

Bible Belt can be offensive to many people, so use it with care.

biblical references. In citing passages from the Bible, use book, chapter, and verse (roman type, no abbreviations): 2 Chronicles 7:14; Proverbs 3:5-6; Psalms 23:1-6, but the 23rd Psalm.

biennial. Every two years. For twice a year, use biannual or semiannual.

big bang, big-bang theory

big government

Big Two (Three, Four, etc.). Use expressions like *Big Oil* only when the article makes clear what is meant.

bill. Lowercase for legislation, even when used with popular names that are capitalized because they might be unclear in themselves: clean-air bill, Levin-Mikulski bill, the Sunshine in Government bill, but GI Bill, Bill of Rights.

billion. Abbreviation, bil., is acceptable in charts, maps, and tables. See MILLION.

Bill of Rights. Capitalize when referring to the first 10 amendments to the U.S. Constitution; lowercase otherwise: a patients' bill of rights.

bimonthly. Once every two months. For twice a month, write semimonthly.

bishop. Capitalize before a name; lowercase otherwise: Bishop Karl Haas (Bishop Haas, the bishop), Suffragan Bishop George Manship (the suffragan bishop).

biweekly. Once every two weeks. For twice a week, write semiweekly.

black. African-American, Afro-American, and black are acceptable as synonyms, but take personal preference of individuals being described into account when applying a term to them. See RACIAL DESIGNATIONS.

black caucus, but Congressional Black Caucus

Black Muslim should be used only as a historical term or when quoting someone. See ISLAM and MUSLIM.

blastoff (noun), blast off (verb)

block/bloc. When referring to a political alignment, use *bloc:* The legislation passed with the help of the labor bloc, but The block of votes from labor was all that was needed.

blond (noun and adjective, male and female)

bluebook. A student examination booklet.

blue book. An official government report or a social registry.

Blue Cross and Blue Shield Association, but check individual organizations, which use a variety of styles for their names.

blue ribbon (noun), blue-ribbon (adjective)

board. Capitalize in a name; lowercase when alone and in generic references: Federal Reserve Board (the board), the Lynn County Board of Regents (the board of regents), Microsoft's board of directors.

boatlift (noun). A system of moving people by boat.

boat lift (noun). A device that raises boats from the water.

boatyard

bobby socks (noun)

bobby-sox (adjective), bobby-soxer (noun)

Bohemian. Capitalize in references to Bohemia; lowercase in references to lifestyle.

bold names. Use boldface for most punctuation that follows boldfaced names, as in Whispers and People files. Exceptions are parentheses, brackets, and 's possessives: Most preferred **Garry Trudeau,** but **Al Capp**'s fans nominated others (**Jeff MacNelly, Lynn Johnston,** and **Pat Oliphant**) for the honor. Titles and the personified Whispers are lightface roman: Treasury Secretary **Dylan Zgorski** said Whispers had it all wrong.

bond ratings. AAA, AA, BBB+, BB–, etc.

book titles. Set in italics. Capitalize principal words and prepositions and conjunctions of more than three letters. For readability, make all-cap and all-lowercase titles caps and lowercase. For religious books, like the Bible and the Koran, use roman type, with no quotation marks. Do not use a comma between a book title and the author's name: *The Bonfire of the Vanities* by Tom Wolfe. Initial articles may be dropped if the syntax would make a sentence awkward: The film was not faithful to Wolfe's *Bonfire of the Vanities*. Put publication data in parentheses: *Juba to Jive: A Dictionary of African-American Slang* by Clarence Major (Penguin Books, 1994, $14.95). When a copyright notation is called for, use the copyright symbol and the year, separated by a space (© 1997). When the symbol is not available, use Copyright 1997. See TITLES OF WORKS.

border states. See POLITICAL REGIONS.

born-again Christian. Use the term only in connection with people who describe themselves that way. For general descriptions, use words like *evangelical Christian* or *fundamentalist Christian* to distinguish such people from members of other segments of the Christian spectrum.

bounceback (noun), bounce back (verb)

( )bound. Combinations are generally solid, but hyphenate when used with a proper noun: westbound, snowbound, deskbound, dutybound, homewardbound, leatherbound, Washington-bound.

box office (noun and adjective)

boy. Do not use for males 18 and older.

brackets. Use brackets for parenthetical material within parentheses and to enclose explanatory matter that the magazine inserts in letters to the editor, exact texts, or quoted passages: "He stayed through the final meeting [March 26, 1977] before flying home." See PARENTHESES.

Brahman/brahmin. Use Brahman for references to the Hindu caste and the breed of cattle; use brahmin for references to people of long-established culture and wealth: Brahman bull, Boston brahmins.

brain trust, brain truster. Lowercase general references, but capitalize in references to Franklin Roosevelt's advisory group.

brainwash, brainwasher, brainwashing

brand names. See TRADEMARKS.

Brazilian names generally resemble those of the Portuguese. But, because of Brazil's polyglot culture, use extra caution in determining individual usage. If there is doubt about whether to use both parts of a double surname, it is safer to do so. Francisco Thompson Flores Neto (Thompson Flores). *Neto* is not a basic part of the name but an appendage that means grandson.

breeds. Capitalize only proper nouns: Labrador retriever, golden retriever, collie, thoroughbred, standardbred.

Britain consists of England, Scotland, and Wales. The United Kingdom (officially the United Kingdom of Great Britain and Northern Ireland) is Britain and Northern Ireland. The British Isles consist of Britain, Ireland, and adjacent islands, including the Isle of Man and the Channel Islands.

British Columbia. Abbreviate, B.C., only in charts, maps, and tables.

British Columbian

British spellings. Use U.S. spellings for generic words that are part of proper names unless the British spelling is also used in America as an alternative spelling: the British Labor Party, Britain's Ministry of Defense, but the Barbican Centre.

British thermal unit. See BTU.

brokerage means "the business or office of a broker," so *brokerage firm* is redundant.

Brothers. In company names, capitalize and spell out or abbreviate as the company does. Bro. and Bros. are acceptable in charts and tables.

brunet (noun and adjective, male and female)

brush fire (noun), brush-fire (adjective)

brussels sprouts

Btu. Abbreviation for British thermal unit, acceptable on all references when the meaning is clear: 25 Btu, a 500-Btu air conditioner.

budget, federal

buildings. Capitalize names: the Empire State Building; his home, Dunrovin; the Zambian Embassy (the embassy); the U.S. Capitol (the Capitol).

bull market (noun), bull-market (adjective)

bureau. Capitalize when part of an official name; lowercase otherwise: the Bureau of Land Management, the Bureau of the Census, the Census Bureau, the bureau, *Rolling Stone*'s Chicago bureau.

bus (buses)/**buss** (busses). A bus is a vehicle; buss is a kiss or to kiss.

businessman, businesswoman, but small-business man. Consider using gender-neutral alternatives, like businessperson, business people, business executive.

( )buster. Write solid: broncobuster, crimebuster, budgetbuster.

buyback

buyer's market

bylines. For byline spelling and initials, follow the masthead; for stringers' names, consult the "domstrings-usn-usn" and "forstrings-usn-usn" electronic files. Sign editor's notes *–The Editor* in italics at the end of the note. When the signature is on a line by itself, set it flush right. When using initials as a story credit, use a thin space, an en dash, periods, italics, and no spaces between the initials: *–R.J.N.* When possible, avoid breaking names over a line in byline tags.

Byzantine. Capitalize references to Byzantium or the Byzantine Empire; lowercase references to complex or devious political situations.

CAT scan

cabinet. Lowercase all uses. See DEPARTMENT.

cabinet departments. Capitalize department names (Department of Labor, Labor Department) and titles when they precede a person's name (Labor Secretary Dahlia Hearst), but lowercase titles otherwise: Dahlia Hearst, the labor secretary. Capitalize the defining department name when it stands alone and when necessary for clarity: New funding for Commerce is actually quite modest, but avoid overusing that construction, which sounds jargonistic.

cabinet members. See TITLES OF PERSONS.

calf's liver

caliber refers to a bullet's diameter, usually measured in hundredths of an inch or millimeters: .22-caliber rifle, 9-mm handgun, .45-caliber pistol, a .45 semiautomatic. See FIREARMS.

California (Calif., CA in addresses)

Californian

call-( ). callback, call-down, call-off, call-out, call-over (all nouns).

calorie(s). Abbreviate, cal., only in charts, maps, and tables.

Canada. See individual entries for provinces and territories.

Canal Zone. Abolished by the Panama Canal treaties, which were ratified in 1978. In historical references, abbreviate, C.Z., only in charts, maps, and tables. Note that it was the Canal Zone, not *the Panama Canal Zone.*

canton. Lowercase except in a name: the canton of Lucerne (the canton); Canton Lake, Okla.

canvas/canvass. Canvas is cloth; canvass is to examine or to seek opinions or support.

capital gains, capital-gains tax

capitalization. *U.S. News* generally uses a "down" style. For most questions, see separate entries in this book and in the electronic NAMES and PLACES lists. For words not covered here or in those places, consult *Webster's New World College Dictionary*.

TERMS DERIVED FROM PROPER NOUNS are usually lowercase when the connection with the proper noun is remote: balkanize, brussels sprouts, caesar salad, chinese checkers, ferris wheel, french fries, india ink, manila folder, molotov cocktail, pyrrhic victory, roman numeral, russian roulette, spartan, swiss steak, thespian, yankee pot roast, but Scotch whisky (it's made only in Scotland).

AFTER A COLON. Capitalize the first word only when it begins a complete sentence, when it would normally be capitalized anyway, or when capitalization is needed for dramatic effect: He put it this way: The answer is final. They found what they had sought: a final answer. He had a single objective: Victory. Depending on the effect desired, the initial word following a colon in a headline may be capped even if it does not begin a complete sentence.

PLURALS. When a common noun follows two or more names with which it is combined, lowercase the noun: the Keystone and Prudential buildings, the Rappahannock and Potomac rivers, Yale and Harvard universities, the State and Interior departments. But when the noun precedes the capitalized names, it is capitalized: the Departments of State and Interior, the Universities of Michigan and California, Mounts Monadnock and McKinley.

SPECIAL EXPRESSION. Capitalizing ordinarily lowercase words to achieve emphasis or irony should generally be avoided in favor of obtaining the same result through sentence structure or italics.

SMALL CAPS, with no quotation marks, may be used for special effect when rendering signs and headlines in body type: The sign read DON'T TREAD ON ME.

BEGINNING OF A SENTENCE. Capitalize the first word of a sentence, even when it is a proper noun that would normally be lowercase: EBay's attorney insisted that eBay would survive the setback. When a small-cap abbreviation begins a sentence, put all the letters in small caps: BET launched three programs. See ABBREVIATIONS, ACRONYMS, AGES AND ERAS, BYLINES, CENTRAL, COLON, GEOGRAPHIC NAMES, GEOGRAPHIC TERMS, GERMAN COMMON NOUNS, HEADLINES, HISTORIC PERIODS, MILITARY TITLES, NAMES OF PERSONS, SMALL CAPS, TITLES OF PERSONS, TRADEMARKS, foreign-names entries, and other individual entries.

captions. STANDARD CAPTIONS are generally flush left. When they contain a complete sentence, they take a period at the end, even if the sentence is followed by a fragment. When they contain no complete sentence, they take no period:

Mideast cafes get some fancy meat choppers.
Snow fell. A quiet night.
A little overdone

TENSE of a caption customarily is the present, even if an event long past is pictured, but avoid absurdities:

Awkward: *Umbrellas leave the factory last July.*
Better: Umbrellas leaving the factory last July

MAPS take the following styling:

ITALIC CAPS AND LOWERCASE	ROMAN CAPS AND LOWERCASE
Gulfs	Cities
Rivers	Canals
Lakes	Railways
Oceans	Highways
Channels	

FULL CAPS, ROMAN	LIGHTFACE CAPS OR SPECIAL STYLING
Planets	Counties
Countries	
States	
Provinces	

IDENTIFICATION. Put location words in parentheses unless the direction is the first word in a sentence:

An undercover FBI agent (left) confronts the suspect.
Above, the president buys a skirt.

Make sure to identify all major figures in a photograph, listing them, all other factors being equal, as they appear left to right.

Officer James Tuite (left) arrests Fred Belanger.

But when the identifications are obvious, location words are superfluous and should not be used:

Holly Hunter greets Dick Cheney at the Watergate.

CARTOON CAPTIONS are usually written with quotation marks. If the original caption is already a quote—indicating, for instance, words spoken by a character in the cartoon—our caption still uses only one set of quotation marks. Use a period. Cartoon captions usually are centered, in caps and lowercase: "A real bad scene." See CHARTS AND TABLES, CREDITS, and FAIRNESS.

carat/caret/karat. Carat is a unit of weight for gemstones; caret is an editing mark showing where material is to be inserted; karat is a measure of gold's purity.

cardholder, but credit-card holder

cardinal. The title comes first: Cardinal John O'Hara, Cardinal O'Hara, the cardinal.

carry back (verb), carry-back (noun and adjective)

carry forward (verb), carry-forward (noun and adjective)

carryout (noun and adjective)

carry over (verb), carry-over (noun and adjective)

cast-iron ware, but ironware

Catholic. Use Roman Catholic, at least on first reference, if that is what is meant. See ROMAN CATHOLIC CHURCH.

CAT scan. See CT SCAN.

caucus. Capitalize in a full name; lowercase otherwise: Congressional Black Caucus, black caucus, the caucus.

CB (noun and adjective). Acceptable for citizens' band radio when the meaning is clear.

CD-ROM. Abbreviation for compact disk–read-only memory. Acceptable on first reference when the meaning is clear.

CDT. See TIME ZONES.

Celsius. 150 degrees Celsius, 48°C. To convert from Fahrenheit, subtract 32, then multiply by five ninths. To convert to Fahrenheit, multiply by 1.8, then add 32.

center on. Don't write *center around*. Use center on, cluster around, etc.

centimeter. Abbreviation, cm, acceptable after first reference and in charts and tables. See METRIC SYSTEM.

central. Capitalize *central, upper, lower,* and *middle* when part of an accepted name; lowercase when merely descriptive: Central America, Central Europe, central North America, Upper Michigan, Upper Peninsula of Michigan, Lower California (for Baja California), Lower East Side (of Manhattan), Middle East, upper Midwest.

Central American (noun and adjective)

century. Lowercase. Spell out under 10: second century, second century B.C., 16th century, the 1600s, 12th-century building.

WHEN CENTURIES BEGIN AND END is an age-old debate. Although common belief holds that the 21st century, for example, began Jan. 1, 2000, many people, reasoning that the first year was A.D. 1, not A.D. 0, insist that it didn't begin until 2001. Writers wishing to avoid an argument should explain both sides or shun the issue altogether.

cesarean section (C-section)

chair. chairman, chairwoman, chairperson. Capitalize before a name; lowercase otherwise: Chairman Tessie Van Landingham of the Senate Banking Committee (Chairman Van Landingham, the chairman). If you know the titleholder's preference on which word to use, follow it; if not, use *chairman* or *chair.*

chamber. Capitalize in the name of an organization; lowercase alone: the Miami Chamber of Commerce (the Chamber of Commerce, the chamber), a chamber of commerce.

channel. Capitalize with a number: Channel 3 (the channel).

chapter. Capitalize with a number; lowercase alone: Chapter 11, Chapter IV (the chapter).

characters in movies, plays, operas, novels, television shows, etc., are set roman, without quotes: Henry Fonda played Mr. Roberts in the movie version of *Mr. Roberts.*

charter. Capitalize in a name; lowercase otherwise: The United Nations Charter (the charter).

charts and tables. A typical table:

Rural-crop seesaw
Persimmons soar as sorghum sags.

U.S. commodity fluctuations:

	Gain or loss (in tons)	Change
Persimmons	460 mil.	+40%
Sorghum	−13 mil.	−12%

Note: Figures are for fiscal 1990. Source: U.S. Agriculture Dept.

HEADLINE (*Rural-crop seesaw*) may be all caps or caps and lowercase.

CHATTER (*Persimmons soar as sorghum sags.*). Capitalize the first word and proper nouns. Use a final period when the chatter is a complete sentence, no period when it is a fragment.

LABEL (*U.S. commodity fluctuations:*) ends with a period if it is a sentence and with a dash, colon, ellipsis points, or no punctuation if it is not.

COLUMN HEADLINES (*Gain or loss*). Capitalize the first word. Lowercase parenthetical notes (*in tons*).

STUBS (*Persimmons*) and BODY (*460 mil.*). Capitalize the first word and proper nouns.

PLOTTING LABELS (titles characterizing graph lines or bar charts, etc., usually standing nearby in a strategic place) are caps and lowercase.

ABBREVIATIONS, such as *mil.* and *bil.*, are lowercase. *Dept.* is acceptable in credit lines.

PARALLELISM is desirable in line headings. Treat similar items the same way: *printers, mechanics, and painters*, not *printers, garages, and painters.*

KICKERS, notes, and credits on charts are not indented. Notes and footnotes end with periods. Credits and source lines do not. See ABBREVIATIONS, CREDITS, FOOTNOTES, PERCENT, PERCENTAGE POINT, PERIOD, and SOURCE LINES.

chat room

chemicals. Use subscripts in formulas: CO_2.

Chicano is acceptable to some Mexican-Americans, but use care when referring to individuals, who may object. See HISPANIC and LATINO.

chief justice. Capitalize before a name; lowercase otherwise: Chief Justice William Rehnquist (the chief justice). **Note:** The title is chief justice of the United States, not *chief justice of the Supreme Court.*

chief of staff. Capitalize before a name; lowercase otherwise: White House Chief of Staff Andrew Card, Chief of Staff Andrew Card, the chief of staff.

Chinese names. The two primary systems for transliterating Chinese are Pinyin and Wade-Giles. Pinyin is used throughout the mainland and has become the spelling of record in Western academic works and in the Western press. Wade-Giles is still used by many nonmainland Chinese, in Taiwan, and in Singapore. Chinese names consist of a family name (almost always one syllable) followed by one or two given names. For subsequent references, only the family name need be used: Deng Xiaoping (Deng), Li Peng (Li). However, if a story refers to several people with the same family name, for example, Li Peng and Li Xiannian, the whole name should be repeated. In Wade-Giles, given names are hyphenated (Teng Hsiao-p'ing); in Pinyin, they are not (Deng Xiaoping). Use Pinyin spellings except for individuals whose preference for another spelling is known, for certain well-known historical figures, and for certain well-known place names: Sun Yat-sen, Chiang Kai-shek (historical); Tibet, Mongolia, Taipei (well-known place names). Some Chinese, especially those who live in or have been educated in the West, have westernized their names, putting the family name last: Stephen Soo-ming Lo (Lo), James C. H. Shen (Shen).

PLACE NAMES: Tiananmen Square, Beijing (**not Peking**), Guangzhou (**not Canton**), Chongqing (**not Chungking**), Nanjing (**not Nanking**), Yan'an (**not Yenan**), Shanxi province (**not Shansi**), Shaanxi province (**not Shensi**), Jiangsu province (**not Kiangsu**), Xinjiang autonomous region (**not Sinkiang**).

DYNASTIES: Qing dynasty (**not Ch'ing**), Tang dynasty (**not T'ang**), Zhou dynasty (**not Chou**). See electronic NAMES and PLACES lists.

chlorofluorocarbons. The abbreviation, CFCs, is acceptable on first reference when the meaning is clear.

chord/cord. A chord is a combination of musical notes; a cord is a thin rope, a measure of wood, or vocal tissue.

Christmas Eve

church. Capitalize in names of denominations and names of individual churches; lowercase alone: the Episcopal Church (the church), Grace and Holy Trinity Episcopal Church (the church), an Episcopal church, the Episcopal church next door. See DENOMINATIONS and separate entries for particular churches.

Church of Christ, Scientist (Christian Scientists). On subsequent reference, the church. Capstone of the denomination is the Mother Church, named the First Church of Christ, Scientist, in Boston. The Mother Church is run by a five-member board of directors: Jane Anderson, member of the board of directors (Anderson). Local congregations are called branch churches. Their connection is directly with the Mother Church. They operate according to the church manual of the Mother Church, as does the Mother Church itself. Branch churches never use *the* before their names. That is reserved for the Mother Church. A local church would be: First (Second, Third, etc.) Church of Christ, Scientist (the church). Clerical titles are not used by Christian Scientists. A local congregation may have a first reader and a second reader: Mary Johnson, first reader in Second Church of Christ, Scientist (Johnson). Christian Science practitioners—leaders in the church who pray for healing—work independent of the local churches: John Barton, a Christian Science practitioner (Barton). Lecturers are members of the Board of Lectureship of the Mother Church: Mavis LaPorte, a Christian Science lecturer (LaPorte).

CIA (Central Intelligence Agency) is acceptable on first reference when the meaning is clear.

Circle. Spell out and capitalize in a mailing address; lowercase alone. See ADDRESSES.

cities. Whether the name of a city can be used by itself, without an identifying state or country, varies with the article's context and the flow of the news. For example, if we are writing about the Southern United States, we may not need to include *Fla.* with *St. Petersburg;* if we are writing about European politics, we could write *St. Petersburg* without adding *Russia.* A story about the movie industry could have *Hollywood* without *Calif.,* and in an article about the Pacific Northwest, *Portland* could stand without *Ore.*

In general, the cities below do not need to be followed by a state or a country, but apply common sense in using other names alone or in adding the state or country to any of the cities listed here.

Amsterdam	Cleveland	Madrid	Quebec
Anchorage	Copenhagen	Memphis	Rio de Janeiro
Athens	Dallas	Mexico City	Rome
Atlanta	Denver	Miami	Salt Lake City
Atlantic City	Des Moines	Milwaukee	San Antonio
Austin	Detroit	Minneapolis	San Diego
Baghdad	Dublin	Montreal	San Francisco
Baltimore	Edinburgh	Moscow	Seattle
Barcelona	Florence	Naples	Seoul
Beijing	Fort Worth	Nashville	Shanghai
Beirut	Frankfurt	New Delhi	St. Louis
Berlin	Geneva	New Orleans	Stockholm
Bombay	Havana	New York	Sydney
Bonn	Hong Kong	Oklahoma City	Tampa
Boston	Honolulu	Omaha	Tel Aviv
Brussels	Houston	Orlando	Tokyo
Buenos Aires	Indianapolis	Oslo	Toronto
Buffalo	Istanbul	Ottawa	Venice
Cairo	Jerusalem	Paris	Vienna
Calcutta	Las Vegas	Philadelphia	Warsaw
Cape Town	London	Phoenix	Washington
Chicago	Los Angeles	Pittsburgh	Zurich
Cincinnati			

citizens band radio (CB)

city. Capitalize when part of name; lowercase otherwise: New York City (city of New York, the city), Atlantic City, the City of Brotherly Love, Twin Cities, Baltimore city (when necessary to distinguish it, for instance, from the separate *Baltimore County*), the City (London's financial district).

City Council, the Lodi City Council, the City Council, city councils, the council

civil rights (noun and adjective)

Civil Rights Act of 1991, the Civil Rights Act, a civil rights act

civil service

claim. Do not use as a synonym for *say,* because it may indicate that the writer doubts the truth of what is said. A neutral alternative is *assert.*

class. Capitalize with letter or number: Class II, Class 12, Class A, "L" Class. Lowercase with a year: the class of '64.

claymore mine

club owner

co( ). Generally, write solid: coauthor, coexistence, cofounder, cooperate, coordinate, costar, coworker, coconspirator, but co-op.

coach. Capitalize before a name as a title; lowercase otherwise: Coach Coughlin (the coach).

coalfield, but coal mine, coal miner, coal yard

coast. Lowercase references to shoreline; capitalize references to a region: The Pacific coast is dotted with rocky islands; Pacific Coast industries; Pacific Coast states.

Coast Guard. Capitalize in reference to a particular country's organization: the U.S. Coast Guard (the Coast Guard), but a coast guard, a coast guardsman.

c.o.d. Acceptable for cash on delivery or collect on delivery when the meaning is clear.

code. Capitalize in an official title; lowercase alone and in a general sense: Internal Revenue Code (the revenue code, the code), civil code, Federal Criminal Code.

code-named. Such words are usually roman and capitalized: code-named Popeye.

coed. As an adjective, *coed* can be a useful alternative to coeducational, but as a noun, *student* is usually preferred.

cold-roll (verb)

Cold War (noun and adjective), but cold warrior

College Board. This was known formerly, and in a strictly legal sense is still known, as the College Entrance Examination Board (the board).

colleges and universities. Capitalize college, university, school, academy, institute, etc., when part of a name; lowercase alone: Harvard University (the university), St. John's College (the college), Pratt Institute (the institute), Sharon Hill High School (the high school in Sharon Hill). Capitalize divisions of a college, university, etc., when part of a name; lowercase when expressing a function (departments ordinarily are lowercase on the assumption that the words are functional) and when they are not the official name: Harvard Law School (Harvard's law school, the law school at Harvard), University of Texas School of Law, but University of Texas law school, the Harvard history department, the English department.

ABBREVIATING NAMES. When you must abbreviate in a chart or a table, do so in this order:
1. Abbreviate University as Univ., or U., College as Col., Academy as Acad., and Institute as Inst.
2. Abbreviate Technology as Tech.
3. Use an ampersand for *and.*
4. Abbreviate the name of the state (Univ. of Calif.–Long Beach).
5. When necessary, if the institution's own preferred shortened name is more understandable to readers than the name determined by these rules (Penn State instead of *Pa. State Univ.,* for example), use it. When Tech is used as part of a popular name for the school, drop the period (Georgia Tech).

Example:
Massachusetts Institute of Technology
Massachusetts Inst. of Technology
Massachusetts Inst. of Tech.
Mass. Inst. of Tech.

When using letter abbreviations, write them solid: MIT, UCLA, UNC, but U.Va.

AND/AMPERSAND. Use *and* except with abbreviations: Davis and Elkins College, Texas A&M University.

CAMPUS NAMES. Distinguish a university's campuses from one another by using an en dash between the name of the school and the campus, regardless of whether the school itself uses *in, at,* a dash, a hyphen, parentheses, a virgule, a colon, or nothing between the name and the location (University of Maryland–Baltimore County, University of Maryland–Eastern Shore, State University of New York–Albany, University of

California–Los Angeles). CUNY and SUNY are acceptable in charts and tables for City University of New York and State University of New York, respectively (CUNY–Hunter College, SUNY College–Fredonia).

INDEXING. Use the letter-by-letter system:
Millsaps College
Mills College

Alphabetize names beginning with *St.* as they appear:
Shaw University
St. John's College

Alphabetize abbreviations as they appear:
Stetson University
SUNY–Buffalo
Swarthmore College

Index names beginning with an article, like *the Citadel,* by the first distinguishing name:
Citadel, the

Ignore apostrophes and hyphens in a word:
Dyke College
D'Youville College
Trinity College
Tri-State University

STATES. When locating institutions in text, use traditional state abbreviations (Tenn., Pa., etc.), spelling out Alaska, Hawaii, Idaho, Iowa, Maine, Ohio, Texas, and Utah. Postal Service abbreviations may be used to locate institutions in tables and indexes. Do not use the state abbreviation when the state is included in the name of the institution.

THE. Do not use a capitalized *The* when it appears in front of the name (American University, College of Idaho, Sage Colleges, but College of the Holy Cross, University of the South). In text, use a lowercase *the* with the name when it sounds natural (He attends the University of Pennsylvania, She applied to the Citadel, but She teaches at Pennsylvania State University).

colloquialisms. See SLANG, DIALECT, and JARGON.

colon. Capitalize the first word that follows a colon when the word begins a complete sentence, is a proper noun, would ordinarily be capitalized, or needs to be capitalized for dramatic effect. The first word following a colon in a headline may be capped or not depending on the effect desired. A colon may be used:

TO INTRODUCE QUOTED MATERIAL: The president said: "I have absolutely no comment."

TO INTRODUCE A SHORT OR LONG PASSAGE either in or out of quotation marks:
The following message was E-mailed from Madrid:
The text of Jefferson's address follows:

TO INTRODUCE A SERIES: Austria faces three pressing problems: unemployment, galloping inflation, and spiritual malaise.

TO SEPARATE THE CLAUSES of a compound sentence when the second clause is an illustration, an explanation, or a restatement of the first: Carter had a drawback: He could not win the golf vote.

AVOID OVERUSING colons for dramatic effect. In many cases, a comma or semicolon, both of which slow down a reader less than a colon does, will serve just as well. See DASH.

colonies. Capitalize in reference to the 13 that became the United States; lowercase otherwise. Lowercase *colonial.*

Coloradan

Colorado (Colo., CO in addresses)

colored. Acceptable for references to certain South Africans of racially mixed parentage, but only in quotes and with an explanation.

comandante. Spanish military title. Set in italics, but make it roman when it is capped before a name.

comet. Hale-Bopp comet. See heavenly bodies.

comic books. Put titles in italics: *Wonder Woman.*

comic strips. Put titles in italics: *Doonesbury.*

comma. Commas are used to identify and separate the parts of sentences, clauses, and phrases. In some cases, the comma can be omitted without harm. It is sometimes inserted where not needed structurally but where a pause is desired for clarity—which often means the sentence is awkward and should be rewritten.

COORDINATE CLAUSES in a compound sentence are usually separated by a comma: The premier resigned, and the king fled. In a short sentence of that type, where clarity is not diminished, the comma can be left out: The premier resigned and the king fled. But in a long compound sentence, or a short one where confusion might arise, the comma may be essential. Incorrect: *Jones murdered Smith and Anderson robbed a bank.* (Until the reader readjusts at the word *robbed,* the impression is that Jones murdered Smith and Anderson. A comma is needed.)

SUBORDINATE CLAUSES are usually set off by commas when they appear before the main clause. These commas may sometimes be omitted: Although commas are useful, they may sometimes be omitted. Although commas are useful they may sometimes be omitted.

DESCRIPTIVE CLAUSES AND APPOSITIVES are set off by commas: Senator Blank, who drives a Jaguar, opposes a duty on autos. Her husband, Tom, arrived. (She has only one husband.)

RESTRICTIVE CLAUSES AND APPOSITIVES are not set off by commas: The man who said that was undermining foreign policy. Your January 14 article "Whither Dithers?" was terrific. (There was more than one article dated January 14.) Her sister Whitney went home (when she has more than one sister).

INTRODUCTORY WORDS AND PHRASES are usually set off by commas: Finally, police used dogs to control the students. Such commas can sometimes be omitted without damage: Yet advisers were perplexed.

PARENTHETICAL WORDS, phrases, or clauses are usually set off by commas: Subordinate clauses, likewise, are set off. Or: Subordinate clauses likewise are set off. A vote of no confidence, he said, would mean ruin. After *and, but,* or *that* at the beginning of a sentence or clause, the comma before the parenthetical matter may be omitted if the sentence remains clear: And[,] for all I know, she may never return. It is clear that[,] when all is said and done, the fat man has sung.

ITEMS IN A SERIES are divided by commas: On his farm he grew soybeans, peanuts, and corn. Larry couldn't decide whether to fire Hank, promote Artie, or drop the matter altogether.

WHERE WORDS ARE OMITTED, commas may be substituted: Mikulski won 42 percent of the vote; Guercio, 23 percent. Note, however, that if the parts are short and the connection is clear, the commas showing omissions are not mandatory: Mikulski won 42 percent of the vote, Guercio 23 percent.

A PERSON'S RESIDENCE OR WORKPLACE is usually not set off by commas:
Tim Connolly of the Budd Co. said . . .
Gov. Rex Denzer of Arkansas said . . .
Senator Allison of North Dakota asked . . .

BEFORE ZIP CODES, no comma is used: Washington, DC 20037.

PLUS does not require a preceding comma unless the cadence and structure of the sentence call for it:
Intelligence plus luck pulled him through.
Intelligence, plus a strong element of luck, won out.

OTHER USES of the comma:
On Nov. 18, 1906, he was born.
In April 1977, she shot a bear.
Rockford, Ill.
4,760,200
2400 N Street NW, Washington, DC 20037

OVERUSE of commas can be destructive. Since the function of the comma is to break up a sentence into parts whose relationships are clear, insertion of additional commas may confuse the relationships. Incorrect: *When the best farmland is converted to other purposes, agriculture is forced to use less productive acreage, and the cost of food production rises.* Everything after the first comma is part of what happens when the best land is converted. The second comma should be omitted. Incorrect: *To ease the strain on pinched borrowers, credit companies, banks, and finance houses have stretched out payment schedules.* The first comma sets out the purpose of the action told in the second part of the sentence. But the commas in the series are piled on, making it seem that pinched borrowers, credit companies, banks, etc., are all parts of the same series. Since the structure of the sentence creates this problem, rewriting is necessary: Credit companies, banks, and finance houses have stretched out payment schedules to ease the strain on pinched borrowers.

NOT ONLY . . . Do not use a comma in such sentences as She found that he was not only a liar but also a cheat unless the two parts form a compound sentence or confusion would otherwise result.

WITH FIGURES. Commas are normally used every three digits to the left of a decimal point (1,500 pounds, 1,000,250 votes). Exceptions include: stock market indexes, years, addresses, page numbers, chapters of fraternal organizations and labor unions, serial numbers, numbers to the right of decimals, and test scores. But when numbers for indexes and years contain five or more digits, use a comma: the Nasdaq approached 3200

while the Nikkei broke 17,800; A.D. 1964; 12,500 B.C. **See** DASH and
SEMICOLON.

commander in chief. Capitalize before a name; lowercase otherwise: Commander in Chief Mark Schwartz, Commander in Chief Schwartz, the commander in chief.

commission. Capitalize in a name; lowercase alone: Federal Communications Commission (the commission), Fulton County Commission (the
commission), the Fulton County commissioners.

commissioner. Capitalize when used as a title before a name. Descriptive
qualifiers are usually lowercase: baseball Commissioner Jamal Jones,
county Commissioner Christine Cedar.

committee. Capitalize in names of official groups and in names of organizations; lowercase alone, in names of ad hoc groups, in names of com-
mittees of organizations, and in plurals: the House Banking and Financial Services Committee (the Banking Committee, the committee), the
Senate committee that deals with postal affairs, the Committee for Economic Development, the national committee, the team's membership committee, the finance committee of the Democratic National Committee.

Commons. Capitalize references to the British House of Commons.

common-stock holder, but stockholder

communication/communications. The first refers to the act of commu-
nicating, the second to equipment, the industry, etc.

Communion. Capitalize in reference to the Eucharist: Holy Communion,
Communion. **Also,** the Lord's Supper.

communism

Communist. Capitalize when referring to a particular party; lowercase
in general references: Communist Party official, the Communist foreign
secretary, a Communist, communist ideals.

compact disk. CD is acceptable when the meaning is clear.

company. Abbreviate and capitalize as part of a name; lowercase alone:
Ford Motor Co. (the company). **But spell out** *company* when it comes

at the beginning of a name, when it is plural, and when it is in the name of a military unit: Company B (the company), Anheuser-Busch Companies, Bravo Company. *Co.* is not always needed if the reference is clear: Soundwaves Co. (Soundwaves). Use an ampersand, not *and:* E. I. du Pont de Nemours & Co. See COMPANY NAMES and CORPORATION.

company names. Abbreviate and capitalize *Co.*, *Corp.*, *Inc.*, and *Ltd.* and write them without commas. *Inc.*, *Ltd.*, and *LP* are not necessary if *Co.*, *Corp.*, *Railroad*, *Sons,* or other language makes it clear that a company name is being used. Dow Jones & Co., but Frelinghuysen Chairbottoms Inc., Jesse Filbert Ltd.

ABBREVIATIONS. *Bro.* and *Bros.* may be used in charts, maps, and tables. *Co.* and *Corp.* are not always necessary if the name is familiar and the context is clear. Ford Motor (Ford), Microsoft, and General Electric are usually acceptable. Foreign abbreviations, such as GmbH, AG, OHG, KG, and SA, are usually unnecessary. When abbreviating a company's name with initials on subsequent reference, omit periods unless they are part of the official name: Johnson Rotary Pump Co. (JRP), J.R.P. Co. (J.R.P.).

AND/AMPERSAND. Use an ampersand in all names of business and legal firms, including savings and loan associations, even when the company prefers *and*.

ALL-CAPS NAMES. When a company with an all-caps name pronounces the name by its letters, capitalize all the letters (CSX Corp.), but when the name is not pronounced by its letters and the letters do not stand for anything, capitalize only the first letter (Rand).

THE. Capitalize *the* only in official or formal contexts: The Gap (in a chart), the Gap (in body type).

INTERCAPS AND OTHER AFFECTATIONS. In general, follow copy on names, even when they are unconventional (eBay, Yahoo!). But when a name with a lowercase first letter begins a sentence, capitalize the first letter: EBay stock split twice. When a name's unconventionality renders it difficult to read, regularize the spelling: Isbister International, not *iS-BiSTER International*.

compare to, compare with. Use *compare to* when expressing a similarity between things or when putting them in the same category: She compared her backhand to a fireball. Shall I compare thee to a summer's day? Use *compare with* (the far more common usage) when putting things side by side to examine their similarities or differences: He compared Jan's backhand with Jill's. Virtually all numerical comparisons should use *compare with:* The business earned $14,000 this year, compared with $9,000 last year.

compass directions. Spell out and lowercase when they indicate mere direction or location: The balloon headed east; He worked in eastern Virginia; northeastern Nebraska; western Africa, eastern United States. Capitalize in names; when used alone to designate portions of the world, the continents, nations, and states; and when they designate specific, recognized places: Eastern Hemisphere, East Tennessee, North Korea, Northern Virginia, West Texas, West Africa, Southern California, South Side (of Chicago). The presidential candidates campaigned heavily in the South; Southwest Pacific; West Bank (of the Jordan); Middle East; Mideast; Far East; East bloc (referring to the former Warsaw Pact nations). When unable to determine whether a designation is specific and recognized, use lowercase. Capitalize adjectives when referring to a region's people or characteristics: Southern customs, Midwestern farmers, Western allies, Eastern Europe (in a political rather than a geographic sense). Abbreviate only in charts, maps, tables, and addresses: E., W., S.E., N.N.W., etc.

compose/comprise. The parts compose (or make up) the whole. The whole comprises (or is composed of or is made up of) the parts.

compound sentences. They usually take commas but in some cases need not. See COMMA.

compound words. In deciding whether to make a compound hyphenated, one word with no hyphen, or two words, use the following resources in this order:
1. Entries in this book, including the electronic HYPHENS, NAMES, and PLACES lists.
2. *Webster's New World, Webster's Third International,* and *Random House Unabridged* dictionaries.
3. The following guidelines:

NOUNS OF THE MOMENT. Don't run words together unless the dictionary or this book allows it: bookshop, drugstore, but pen shop, doughnut store.

COMPOUND MODIFIERS. Some compound modifiers (generally made up of an adjective or adverb and a noun) require a hyphen to avoid being misread: small-animal hospital, strong-defense strategy, toxic-waste dump, primary-care facility; for other compounds, although a hyphen may not be required for clarity, a hyphen is helpful because its omission could be jarring: high-stress job. Some modifiers that are read more easily with a hyphen when used with one noun may not need a hyphen when used in a different, familiar construction: intensive-care study, but intensive care unit; liberal-arts orientation, but liberal arts degree; mutual-fund admirers, but mutual fund salesperson. If an expression is instantly clear without a hyphen, drop it: life insurance policy. If a combination is in quotation marks, use no hyphens: a "pay as you play" saxophone, but if the combination is part of a larger quote, hyphenate it: He called his music store a "pay-as-you-play emporium." Combinations that are hyphenated before nouns should not be hyphenated in the predicate—even when they are hyphenated in the dictionary—when the meaning is clear without a hyphen: He is a part-time employee, but he works part time. She is a well-known singer, but the singer is well known. She has time-consuming hobbies, but her hobbies are time consuming. If the reader would be confused or impeded by an unhyphenated combination in the predicate, keep the hyphen: a high-tech piano, the piano was high-tech; a middle-aged bureaucrat, the bureaucrat was middle-aged; open-minded parents, his parents were open-minded. For compounds that precede the noun, use the following guidelines—

HYPHENATE:

● Compounds made up of an adjective and a noun when it might be ambiguous which of the two nouns the adjective modifies: capital-gains tax, foreign-trade balance, free-trade agreement, frequent-flier bonus, hazardous-waste site, high-court ruling, human-rights abuses, inner-city school, last-minute request, leveraged-buyout firm, low-fat diet, major-medical program, organized-crime group, physical-education class, political-science instructor, primary-care facility, private-property law, public-health policy, public-opinion poll, real-estate broker, but affirmative action program, baby boom generation, box office receipts, bulletin board notice, cable television program, civil rights legislation, class action suit, credit card rate, criminal justice system, financial services firm, gun control bill, heart attack victim, home equity loan, law enforcement agency, liberal arts college, life insurance policy, money market fund, nuclear power plant, trade association newsletter.

● Compounds with a present participle: data-processing field, intelligence-gathering equipment, role-playing technique, computer-manufacturing jobs, executive-recruiting firm, but ever rising deficits.

● Compounds with a past participle: deep-seated anxiety, poverty-stricken family, fine-tuned car, better-educated police, much-needed rest, but just published book, once debated issue.

● Compounds made up of an adjective and a noun to which *d* or *ed* has been added: Democratic-controlled Congress, old-fashioned views, able-bodied worker.

● Compounds made up of *well* or *ill* and an adjective: well-worn jeans, ill-gotten gains.

● Most compounds with a number or ordinal as the first element: 20th-century painting, 7-inch scar, second-grade students, first-quarter profit, third-highest mountain, **but** 10 percent reduction, $100 million aircraft.

● Most compounds made up of more than two elements: most-favored-nation status, once-in-a-lifetime opportunity, early-20th-century artist, **but** master of arts degree. When such constructions become cumbersome (*capital-gains-tax cut*), consider moving the modifier to follow the noun: a cut in the capital-gains tax.

● Compounds denoting color: bluish-green water, blue-green algae, bright-yellow wall, black-and-white photo. **Drop the hyphen after the predicate unless the elements are two colors in the same form:** The water was bluish green. The wall was bright yellow. The dress was blue-green.

DO NOT HYPHENATE:

● Combinations formed with *very, ever,* and *once* and with adverbs ending in *ly:* very tight jeans, ever tighter circle, once reliable source, carefully chosen words, poorly reasoned argument. **But when the first word is an adjective ending in *ly*, use a hyphen:** scholarly-journal article, hourly-pay issue.

● Compounds with a letter or numeral as the second element: Type A behavior, Chapter 11 bankruptcy.

● Compounds derived from foreign expressions: ad hoc committee, a priori logic, **but** laissez-faire attitude.

● Compounds that are chemical terms: sodium chloride solution.

● Compounds that are proper nouns: Dead Sea salt, Third World debate, Pulitzer Prize committee, **but** Pulitzer Prize-winning author.

● Compounds with a comparative or superlative adjective: a most thoughtful observer, a less informed source, a more recent photograph. **But exceptions may be made when ambiguity might result without the hyphen:** higher-scoring player, more-hazardous substances, more-affordable houses. **See** HEADLINES **and** HYPHEN.

computer tools, names of. Set roman, no quotes: Excel for Windows, WordPerfect 5.1, Lotus 1-2-3, Release 2.2, Windows, DOS 6, Yahoo!

conference. Capitalize as part of full official name; lowercase when the accompanying word or words are only a place name or a place name and a date. Do not capitalize when accompanied by descriptive words that do not make up an official title; sometimes mere descriptions are inadvertently raised to official status. Borderline cases will require some judgment: the Geneva conference of 1954; in 1954, the Geneva conference on Far Eastern affairs; the International Conference on Extermination of Rats (the world conference on rodents, the conference).

confidant (male and female)

confirmation. See SACRAMENTS.

Congress. Capitalize in reference to U.S. Congress and to the official name of a foreign legislative body. In references such as Congress of Vienna, lowercase congress by itself.

congressional. Capitalize in the name of a district; lowercase otherwise: Third Congressional District, 15th Congressional District, the congressional district, a congressional mandate.

Congressional Black Caucus, but black caucus, the caucus

congressperson, congressman, and congresswoman are not synonyms for member(s) of the House; senators also are congresspersons. The words can be used for a group of members of Congress, in whichever house, although in practice they most often designate House members. Follow an individual's preference on whether to use member of Congress, representative, congressperson, congressman, or congresswoman. See PARTY DESIGNATION.

Connecticut (Conn., CT in addresses)

Connecticuter

conservative. Capitalize when referring to a political party; lowercase when designating a person's political faith: the Conservative Party platform, the Conservatives, a conservative point of view. Since the term often reflects the writer's individual judgment and may not correspond to another writer's interpretation or a reader's, it is best to reserve it for cases on which there is widespread agreement. Where feasible, be more specific: Senator Shawker, who has usually voted with the opponents of abortion . . . .

Constitution. Capitalize in a name and alone when referring to a specific national or state constitution: the U.S. Constitution (the Constitution), the French Constitution (the Constitution), the Arkansas Constitution (the Constitution), the New Mexico and Colorado constitutions, Albania's proposed constitution, a constitution, a constitutional question, a question of constitutionality.

consulate. Capitalize in a name; lowercase alone: the Gambian Consulate, the consulate, the Gambian and French consulates.

consul general. Capitalize when used as a title before a name; lowercase otherwise: Consul General Robert Palmer, the consul general.

consumer price index. CPI is acceptable on second reference.

continent, the. Capitalize when it means Europe: the Continent, but the continent of Europe.

continental United States. Don't use for the states below the Canadian border, because Alaska, too, is on the continent. Say the lower 48, the lower 48 states or the 48 contiguous states.

continual/continuous. Continually means repeatedly; continuously means without interruption.

contractions. Avoid contractions when the meaning is unclear. For example, "The professor insists she's misunderstood" could mean that the professor thinks she is misunderstood or that the professor has misunderstood something.

contrast. As a verb it is usually followed by *with:* Her joy contrasted with his gloom. As a noun, it is usually followed by *between* or *to:* Notice the contrast between her education and his. Her demeanor was in marked contrast to his.

conventions. Capitalize the full name of political conventions: Democratic National Convention, the national convention, the Republican convention, the convention.

convict. Use with regard to criminal, not civil, proceedings. A person could be *convicted* of a sex crime but would be *found liable* in a sex discrimination case. *Found guilty* is similarly incorrect in civil cases.

convince/persuade. Convince should never be followed by an infinitive, but persuade may be: She was convinced that might was right; He was persuaded to give up his gun.

copyright. When a copyright notation is called for, use the copyright symbol and the year, separated by a space: © 2001. When the symbol is not available, use Copyright 2001.

Corn Belt

corporate America

corporation. Abbreviate and capitalize as part of a name, but spell out when it comes at the beginning; spell out and lowercase alone (Palisades Corp., the Corporation for Public Broadcasting, the corporation). *Corp.* is not always needed if the reference is clear. See COMPANY.

corps. Use roman numerals for Army units. Capitalize in a name; lowercase alone: I Corps (the corps), Transportation Corps (the corps), U.S. Army Corps of Engineers (the Corps of Engineers, the corps). See MARINE.

council. Capitalize in the name of an organization or an agency; lowercase in descriptive uses and when alone: the Council on Foreign Relations (the council), the Boise City Council (the City Council, the council), executive council of the AFL-CIO, U.N. Security Council (the Security Council, the council).

councilor/counselor. A councilor is a member of a council; a counselor is one who gives advice.

count. See NOBILITY.

counter( ). Combines solid except before a capitalized word.

countries. Use it and its, not *she* and *her*.

countries, names of. Spell out where possible, even on maps. For a list of abbreviations that may be used in tight situations, see NATIONS AND REGIONS.

county. Capitalize when part of a name; lowercase otherwise: Sawicki County (the county of Sawicki, the county), the county government, Sawicki and Miller counties. Irish: County Cork (the county).

couple usually takes a plural verb: The couple were married in their living room. A couple of songs are enough. But when it is used to signify a single unit, it takes a singular verb: Every couple is expected to lead one dance.

course titles. Capitalize: Physics 202, but a physics course, a physics major.

coursework

court. Capitalize in an official name as well as in shortened names; lowercase alone or when used descriptively: the United States Supreme Court (the Supreme Court, the high court, the court), the United States Court of Appeals for the First Circuit (the U.S. Court of Appeals, the First Circuit Court of Appeals, the First Circuit, the Court of Appeals, the appeals court, the circuit court, the court), the United States District Court, (the district court), the Arkansas Supreme Court (the Supreme Court, the court), the Municipal Court of Chicago (the court), the Circuit Court of Montgomery County (the court), France's Court of Cassation (the court). Most 17-year-olds when arrested are sent to juvenile court. See SUPREME COURT.

court cases. Italicize: *Brunowski v. Minnesota.*

cq. This note in copy means either that the preceding word or passage has been checked or that the writer or editor knows that the preceding word or passage appears wrong but that the usage is intentional: Carol Jonnes [spelling cq] went first.

crackdown (noun), crack down (verb)

( )craft. Combinations are usually solid: spycraft, stagecraft, winecraft.

credits are usually all caps. All photographs must be credited, including corporate publicity photographs, unless specifically noted otherwise by the photography editor. Follow rules for regular copy as to use of italics, quotation marks, accent marks, and abbreviations. Credits for staff photographers, contract photographers, and syndicated photographers on assignment for *U.S. News* take the following style:

JEFFREY MACMILLAN FOR *USN&WR*
ANNIE LIEBOVITZ FOR *USN&WR*
KEN SMITH—SYGMA FOR *USN&WR*

PICKUPS. For syndicated photographers whose work is being picked up, use: KEN SMITH—SYGMA.

AGENCIES. When a photographer and an agency are credited together, use a dash to link them. This makes the hyphen available for use in a compound name: WOLFF—BLACK STAR, HENRI CARTIER-BRESSON—MAGNUM. The names of two agencies given credit for the same photograph are separated by a slash. For credits 5 points and smaller, flank the slash with thin spaces (shift/ctrl spacebar): CONTACT / CAMP.

MORE THAN ONE. When a photographer is credited with more than one photograph on a page, you may indicate that by adding the number of photographs in parentheses: JEFFREY MACMILLAN FOR *USN&WR* (3). Alternatively, when one photographer supplies all the photographs for a given page or up to four pages, you may use: PHOTOGRAPHS BY ASHLEY DELOS FOR *USN&WR.* When one photographer provides all the photographs for a larger package and when a photographer is credited in the story's byline instead of elsewhere, the style is: PHOTOGRAPHY BY ASHLEY DELOS FOR *USN&WR.*

ALTERED PHOTOGRAPHS. For photographs that have been changed manually, use: PHOTO ILLUSTRATION BY LANGSTON CARTER FOR *USN&WR.* Photographs altered by computer techniques should take one of the following credits, depending upon the result: DIGITALLY ALTERED PHOTOGRAPH BY LAKISHA BROOKS FOR *USN&WR,* DIGITAL PHOTO MONTAGE BY LEE CHIN FOR *USN&WR,* CARTER RUSTIN—AP (DIGITALLY RETOUCHED).

ILLUSTRATION AND GRAPHICS CREDITS are slightly different from those for photographs. Credits for illustrations by staffers use a dash between the name and *USN&WR,* while credits for nonstaffers use *for:*
ROB KEMP— *USN&WR* (staff artist)
ELWOOD H. SMITH FOR *USN&WR* (outside artist)

POSITIONS FOR CREDITS are indicated by page layouts. When a credit is not located next to the work it identifies, include words making clear what the credit relates to: ILLUSTRATION BY SUZANNE MARIE FOR *USN&WR.*

CARTOONS. Note variations in the wording of cartoon credits: OLIPHANT FOR UNIVERSAL PRESS SYNDICATE, LURIE IN *ASAHI SHIMBUN.* Some cartoonists and photographers require the use of a copyright symbol. Cartoons take credits whether or not the signature is legible.

NAMES of cartoonists, illustrators, photographers, agencies, and newspapers can be checked with the Photography Department, in the electronic CREDITS list, or, in many cases, in the *Editor & Publisher International Year Book.*

COVER CREDITS. COVER: Photograph by Jeff Doda—Sygma
COVER: Illustration by Doug Johnson   Design: WBMG

COMBINATIONS. ARCHITECT: JAMES BAINBRIDGE; PHOTOGRAPH: RACHEL WATERS

MULTIPLE CREDITS. Put the location in parentheses before the credits: PHOTOGRAPHS (FROM LEFT): BILL AUTH FOR *USN&WR*; DOUG STONE— AP; AFP. But when the location begins the credit, drop the parentheses: CLOCKWISE, TOP TO BOTTOM: NELSON CARTER FOR *USN&WR*; AP; AFP; GAMMA LIAISON. See BYLINES, CAPTIONS, CHARTS AND TABLES, and COPYRIGHT.

criminologist/criminalist. A criminologist studies crime as a social phenomenon; a criminalist is a forensic investigator.

criteria. The singular is criterion; don't write *a criteria.*

cross( ). For spelling, follow the dictionary: cross section, cross-stitch, crosshatch, crossfire. Hyphenate made-up combinations.

crucifixion. Capitalize references to the biblical event; lowercase otherwise: The Crucifixion is a tenet of Christian faith. The senator called the hearings "a crucifixion by the media."

Crusades, Crusaders. Capitalize references to the 11th-, 12th-, and 13th-century military expeditions to Palestine. Lowercase otherwise.

CST. See TIME ZONES.

CT scan. Acceptable for "computed tomography scan" when clear. Also called CAT (computerized axial tomography) scan. (The American College of Radiology prefers CT to CAT and *computed* to *computerized.*) Either is acceptable.

cultural designations. In general, capitalize when referring to a specific style; lowercase in descriptive references: a Baroque opera, but a baroque skateboard. Follow the dictionary for terms not listed individually in this book.

Cultural Revolution. Capitalize when referring to China's Great Proletarian Cultural Revolution; lowercase otherwise.

currencies. Information about the world's currencies is kept up to date by three periodicals: *International Financial Statistics,* published monthly by the International Monetary Fund; *Monthly Bulletin of Statistics,* published by the United Nations; and *Statistical Release H-10,* issued weekly by the Federal Reserve Board. (EC dollars are those issued by the Eastern Caribbean Central Bank; CFA francs are issued by the African Financial Community.)

COUNTRY OR REGION	BASIC UNIT	CHIEF FRACTIONAL UNIT
Afghanistan	afghani	pul(s)
Albania	lek(s)	qintar(s)
Algeria	dinar(s)	centime(s)
American Samoa	dollar(s)	cent(s)
Andorra	French franc(s) and	centime(s)
	Spanish peseta(s)	céntimo(s)
Angola	kwanza(s)	lwei(s)
Anguilla	EC dollar(s)	cent(s)
Antigua and Barbuda	EC dollar(s)	cent(s)
Argentina	peso(s)	centavo(s)
Armenia	dram(s)	luma(s)
Aruba	guilder(s)	cent(s)
Australia	dollar(s)	cent(s)
Austria	schilling(s)	groschen
Azerbaijan	manat	gapik
Bahamas	dollar(s)	cent(s)
Bahrain	dinar(s)	fils
Bangladesh	taka	paisa (paise)
Barbados	dollar(s)	cent(s)
Belarus	ruble(s)	kopeck(s)
Belau	U.S. dollar(s)	cent(s)
Belgium	franc(s)	centime(s)
Belize	dollar(s)	cent(s)
Benin	CFA franc(s)	centime(s)
Bermuda	dollar(s)	cent(s)
Bhutan	ngultrum(s)	chetrum(s)
Bolivia	boliviano(s)	centavo(s)
Bosnia and Herzegovina	dinar(s)	para(s)

COUNTRY OR REGION	BASIC UNIT	CHIEF FRACTIONAL UNIT
Botswana	pula	thebe
Brazil	real(s)	centavo(s)
Britain	pound(s)	penny (pence)
British Virgin Islands	U.S. dollar(s)	cent(s)
Brunei	dollar(s)	cent(s)
Bulgaria	lev(a)	stotinka (stotinki)
Burkina Faso	CFA franc(s)	centime(s)
Burma	kyat(s)	pya(s)
Burundi	franc(s)	centime(s)
Cambodia	riel(s)	sen
Cameroon	CFA franc(s)	centime(s)
Canada	dollar(s)	cent(s)
Cape Verde	escudo(s)	centavo(s)
Cayman Islands	dollar(s)	cent(s)
Central African Republic	CFA franc(s)	centime(s)
Chad	CFA franc(s)	centime(s)
Chile	peso(s)	centesimo(s)
China	yuan	fen
Colombia	peso(s)	centavo(s)
Comoros	franc(s)	centime(s)
Congo, Democratic Republic of	zaire(s)	likuta (makuta)
Congo, Republic of the	CFA franc(s)	centime(s)
Costa Rica	colón(s)	céntimo(s)
Croatia	kuna	lipa
Cuba	peso(s)	centavo(s)
Cyprus	pound(s)	cent(s)
Czech Republic	koruna(s)	haler(s)
Denmark	krone(r)	ore
Djibouti	franc(s)	centime(s)
Dominica	EC dollar(s)	cent(s)
Dominican Republic	peso(s)	centavo(s)
East Timor	U.S. dollar(s)	cent(s)
Ecuador	U.S. dollar(s)	cent(s)
Egypt	pound(s)	piaster(s)
El Salvador	colón(s)	centavo(s)
Equatorial Guinea	CFA franc(s)	centime(s)
Eritrea	birr	cent(s)
Estonia	kroon(s)	sent(s)
Ethiopia	birr	cent(s)
European Union	euro(s)	cent(s)
Falkland Islands	pound(s)	penny (pence)
Fiji	dollar(s)	cent(s)
Finland	markka(a)	penni (pennia)
France	franc(s)	centime(s)

COUNTRY OR REGION	BASIC UNIT	CHIEF FRACTIONAL UNIT
French Guiana	French franc(s)	centime(s)
Gabon	CFA franc(s)	centime(s)
Gambia	dalasi	butut
Georgia	lari(s)	tetri
Germany	deutsche mark(s)	pfennig(s)
Ghana	cedi(s)	pesewa(s)
Greece	drachma(s)	lepton (lepta)
Grenada	EC dollar(s)	cent(s)
Guatemala	quetzal(es)	centavo(s)
Guinea	franc(s)	centime(s)
Guinea-Bissau	CFA franc(s)	centime(s)
Guyana	dollar(s)	cent(s)
Haiti	gourde(s)	centime(s)
Honduras	lempira(s)	centavo(s)
Hong Kong	Hong Kong dollar(s)	cent(s)
Hungary	forint(s)	filler
Iceland	krona (kronur)	eyrir (aurar)
India	rupee(s)	paisa (paise)
Indonesia	rupiah(s)	sen
Iran	rial(s)	dinar(s)
Iraq	dinar(s)	fils
Ireland	pound(s)	penny (pence)
Isle of Man	pound(s)	penny (pence)
Israel	shekel(s)	agora (agorot)
Italy	lira (lire)	centesimo(s)
Ivory Coast	CFA franc(s)	centime(s)
Jamaica	dollar(s)	cent(s)
Japan	yen	sen
Jordan	dinar(s)	fils
Kazakhstan	tenge	tiyn
Kenya	shilling(s)	cent(s)
Kirgizstan	som(s)	tyiyn(s)
Kiribati	Australian dollar(s)	cent(s)
Kuwait	dinar(s)	fils
Laos	kip(s)	at
Latvia	lats	santims (santimi)
Lebanon	pound(s)	piaster
Lesotho	loti (maloti)	lisente
Liberia	dollar(s)	cent(s)
Libya	dinar(s)	dirham(s)
Liechtenstein	litas (litai)	centas (centai)
Luxembourg	franc(s)	centime(s)
Macao	pataca(s)	avo(s)
Macedonia	denar(s)	(none)
Madagascar	franc(s)	centime(s)
Malawi	kwacha	tambala (matambala)

COUNTRY OR REGION	BASIC UNIT	CHIEF FRACTIONAL UNIT
Malaysia	ringgit	sen
Maldives	rufiyaa	lari
Mali	CFA franc(s)	centime(s)
Malta	lira	cent(s)
Marshall Islands	U.S. dollar(s)	cent(s)
Mauritania	ouguiya	khoums
Mauritius	rupee(s)	cent(s)
Mexico	peso(s)	centavo(s)
Micronesia	U.S. dollar(s)	cent(s)
Moldova	leu (lei)	(none)
Monaco	French franc(s)	centime(s)
Mongolia	tugrik(s)	mongo(s)
Morocco	dirham(s)	centime(s)
Mozambique	metical (meticais)	centavo(s)
Namibia	dollar(s)	cent(s)
Nauru	Australian dollar(s)	cent(s)
Nepal	rupee(s)	pice
Netherlands	guilder(s)	cent(s)
New Zealand	dollar(s)	cent(s)
Nicaragua	córdoba(s)	centavo(s)
Niger	CFA franc(s)	centime(s)
Nigeria	naira	kobo
North Korea	won	jeon
Norway	krone(r)	ore
Oman	rial(s)	baiza(s)
Pakistan	rupee(s)	paisa (paise)
Panama	balboa(s)	cent(s)
Papua New Guinea	kina	toea
Paraguay	guaraní(s)	céntimo(s)
Peru	sol(s)	inti(s)
Philippines	peso(s)	centavo(s)
Poland	zloty(s)	grosz(y)
Portugal	escudo(s)	centavo(s)
Puerto Rico	dollar(s)	cent(s)
Qatar	riyal(s)	dirham
Réunion	French franc(s)	centime(s)
Romania	leu (lei)	ban(i)
Russia	ruble(s)	kopeck(s)
Rwanda	franc(s)	centime(s)
Samoa	tala	sene
San Marino	Italian lira (lire)	centesimo(s)
São Tomé and Príncipe	dobra(s)	centave(s)
Saudi Arabia	riyal(s)	halala
Scotland	pound(s)	penny (pence)
Senegal	CFA franc(s)	centime(s)
Seychelles	rupee(s)	cent(s)

COUNTRY OR REGION	BASIC UNIT	CHIEF FRACTIONAL UNIT
Sierra Leone	leone(s)	cent(s)
Singapore	dollar(s)	cent(s)
Slovakia	koruna(s)	haler (haleru)
Slovenia	tolar(s)	stotin(s)
Solomon Islands	dollar(s)	cent(s)
Somalia	shilling(s)	cent(s)
South Africa	rand	cent(s)
South Korea	won	chon
Spain	peseta(s)	céntimo(s)
Sri Lanka	rupee(s)	cent(s)
St. Kitts and Nevis	EC dollar(s)	cent(s)
St. Lucia	EC dollar(s)	cent(s)
St. Vincent and the Grenadines	U.S. dollar(s)	cent(s)
Sudan	pound(s)	piaster
Suriname	guilder(s)	cent(s)
Swaziland	lilangeni (emalangeni)	cent(s)
Sweden	krona (kronor)	ore
Switzerland	franc(s)	centime(s)
Syria	pound(s)	piaster
Taiwan	dollar(s)	cent(s)
Tajikistan	ruble(s)	kopeck(s)
Tanzania	shilling(s)	cent(s)
Thailand	baht(s)	satang
Togo	CFA franc(s)	centime(s)
Tonga	pa'anga	seniti
Trinidad and Tobago	dollar(s)	cent(s)
Tunisia	dinar(s)	millime(s)
Turkey	lira(s)	kurus
Turkmenistan	manat(s)	tenesi
Tuvalu	Australian dollar(s)	cent(s)
Uganda	shilling(s)	cent(s)
Ukraine	hyrvnia (hyrvni)	kopiika (kopiiky)
United Arab Emirates	dirham(s)	fils
Uruguay	peso(s)	centesimo(s)
U.S. Virgin Islands	dollar(s)	cent(s)
Uzbekistan	sum	tiyin
Vanuatu	vatu	centime(s)
Vatican City	lira (lire)	centesimo(s)
Venezuela	bolívar(es)	céntimo(s)
Vietnam	dong	hao
Wales	pound(s)	penny (pence)
Yemen	riyal(s)	fils

COUNTRY OR REGION	BASIC UNIT	CHIEF FRACTIONAL UNIT
Yugoslavia	dinar(s)	para(s)
Zambia	kwacha	ngwee
Zimbabwe	dollar(s)	cent(s)

customs. U.S. Customs Service, the Customs Service, but U.S. customs, a customs declaration, the service.

cut back (verb), cutback (noun and adjective)

cut off (verb), cutoff (noun and adjective)

cyber( ). Solid except before *r* or a capitalization: cyberspace, cybersex, cyber-robot, cyber-Barney.

( ) cylinder. six-cylinder engine, eight cylinders, sixes, eights, V-8, V-6

Czech, Czechoslovak. The Czech and Slovak languages are closely related but distinct from each other. Use Czech when referring to the Czech language, the Czech Republic, and Czech culture before the existence of the Republic of Czechoslovakia (1918-92): The address was broadcast in Czech. She joined the Czech Army in 1993. The Czech composer Smetana relied heavily on folk tunes. Use Slovak similarly. Use Czechoslovak for overall references to the people or former government of Czechoslovakia: The Czechoslovak capital was Prague. Soviet forces arrested 1,500 Czechoslovak citizens.

do's and don'ts

da. See PARTICLES.

Dalai Lama. Capitalize when referring to an individual: The Dalai Lama returned from exile. **Lowercase otherwise:** Who will be the next dalai lama?

dam. Capitalize when part of a name; lowercase otherwise: Grand Coulee Dam (the dam).

dangling modifiers occur when a modifying clause is separated from the thing it modifies, often resulting in a loss of clarity.

CHANGE:

Like many offices across America, Holden's pyrotechnics at the Olympics mesmerized the mailroom at the Hotel California.
TO:
Like many offices across America, the mailroom at the Hotel California was mesmerized by Holden's pyrotechnics at the Olympics.

Dangling from a precipice, my life passed before my eyes.
TO:
As I dangled from a precipice, my life passed before my eyes.

Arriving home after the party, Beethoven's house had been burglarized.
TO:
Arriving home after the party, Beethoven found his house had been burglarized.

Based on the *U.S. News* rankings, I decided to attend the Aruba College of Snorkeling and Philosophy.
TO:
After studying the *U.S. News* rankings, I decided to attend the Aruba College of Snorkeling and Philosophy.

dash. Dashes are used as substitutes for commas, parentheses, colons, and brackets. They are more arresting than commas, but compared with parentheses and brackets they cause less interruption in the flow of copy. As punctuation to introduce a collection of material, they appear more sweeping and less specific than colons. Use an em dash (control/shift/+) in body type, subheads, captions, and precedes. A special, shorter em dash (ctrl/shift/alt/+) is used in headlines and decks. Use the dash to:

SET OFF A PARENTHETICAL EXPRESSION: The race is on—Pride is the favorite—but don't expect any records to be set.

INTRODUCE A SERIES: This year's race includes three Southern candidates—McCool, Wills, and Handley.

INTRODUCE A SECTION or an entire article. It is especially useful to substitute a dash for a colon if the section to follow will itself have sentences or subsections introduced by colons:
Here are reactions around the country—A pipefitter in Sioux City: "I think . . ."

OBTAIN EMPHASIS before a final word, phrase, or clause: One thing he wanted more than any other—to be president. He wanted to win the presidency—and he won it.

TERMINATE AN INTERRUPTED QUOTATION:
What is your greatest ambition, Senator?
As to what I want—
I mean politically, not personally.

But a quote that just trails off should end with an ellipsis and a period:
"I might run," Matthews said, "if . . . ."

CAUTION. Since the dash is more impressive typographically than the comma and a more commanding stop, overuse of dashes is worse than overuse of commas. One dash or pair of dashes is enough for a paragraph, and use in successive paragraphs is often too much. Too many dashes in a single sentence can lead to confusion:
Herbert—the Republican candidate—if she wins in Nebraska—will be a cinch to go all the way. The dashes read like a pair, but they are not.

AN EN DASH (shift/+), longer than a hyphen, half as long as a regular (em) dash, is used as a minus sign; to connect inclusive numbers (1809-65); to connect a college campus name to the parent institution (University of Wisconsin–Madison); and may be substituted for a hyphen in some cases for clarity: Popular Front for the Liberation of Palestine–General Command (PFLP-GC), American Federation of Labor–Congress of Industrial Organizations, white-collar–blue-collar contrast, New York–great-circle route, Minneapolis–St. Paul, Dallas–Fort Worth International Airport. See HYPHEN.

data is plural. Write these data, not *this data.*

datebook

datelines. At the beginning of an article, use small caps and follow with a dash: SIERRA VISTA, ARIZ.—. When used in a byline, follow the style of the byline. See CITIES and entries for each state.

dates. He died Dec. 15, 1955, in Philadelphia; December 15; December 1955; 1950s; 1906–85, but spell out the month on the cover, on the contents page, and in the running foot regardless of length: December 15, 1996. See MONTHS.

day. Capitalize the names of holidays and special days: Election Day, Mother's Day, Inauguration Day, Veterans Day.

Day 1, Day 13, but the 13th day

D-Day

de. See FRENCH NAMES and PARTICLES.

de( ). Generally combines solid except before a capitalized letter or an *e:* de-Stalinization, de-emphasize.

deacon. See entries under individual churches.

death knell

death row

decades. In general, use figures, but spell out when appropriate to the context: '50s, 1950s, lost in the Fifties, 1920s, '20s, Roaring Twenties, mid-'60s.

December. See DATES and MONTHS.

decimals. Use figures. For amounts less than 1, use a 0 before the decimal point if confusion could otherwise result.

Deep South. See POLITICAL REGIONS.

degrees. See TEMPERATURE.

degrees, academic. See BACHELOR OF ARTS DEGREE, JURIS DOCTOR, etc.

deity. Capitalize names of the Supreme Being, names of lesser gods, and appellations meaning God: Allah, God, Jehovah, Yahweh, Holy Ghost, the Almighty, the Father, the King of Kings, the Lamb of God, the Prince of Peace, Apollo, Zeus. **Lowercase pronouns** he, him, etc.

Delaware (Del., DE in addresses)

Delawarean

delegate at large (noun), delegate-at-large (adjective)

deletions. See ELLIPSIS POINTS and QUOTATIONS.

delta. When referring to the Yazoo-Mississippi Delta, the alluvial plain in northwest Mississippi, capitalize all uses: Muddy Waters grew up in the Delta, a Delta bluesman. Otherwise, capitalize when part of a name and lowercase alone: the Mississippi River Delta (at the mouth of the Mississippi—in Louisiana), the delta, the Nile River Delta, the Nile delta.

demi( ). Write solid except before a capitalization or an *i*.

Democratic National Committee (the national committee, the committee, Democratic State Committee)

Democratic National Convention (the national convention, the party convention, the convention)

Democratic Party. Democrats, the party. Abbreviation, Dem. or D, is acceptable only in charts, maps, tables, and parenthetical identifications: Karen Kraft (D-Minn.), but parenthetical IDs should be avoided in regular text. For ways to do so, see PARTY DESIGNATION.

denominations, church. Following are names of some representative denominations from the list of more than 200 published by the National Council of the Churches of Christ in the U.S.A.:

African Methodist Episcopal Church
African Methodist Episcopal Zion Church
American Baptist Churches in the U.S.A.
Assemblies of God
Christian Church (Disciples of Christ)
Christian Churches and Churches of Christ
Church of Christ, Scientist
Church of God in Christ
Church of Jesus Christ of Latter-day Saints
Community of Christ
Episcopal Church
Evangelical Friends International–North America Region

Evangelical Lutheran Church in America
Federation of Reconstructionist Congregations and Havurot
Friends General Conference
Friends United Meeting
Greek Orthodox Archdiocese of America
Hungarian Reformed Church in America
International Pentecostal Holiness Church
Jehovah's Witnesses
Lutheran Church–Missouri Synod
Moravian Church in America
National Baptist Convention of America
National Baptist Convention, U.S.A. Inc.
Orthodox Church in America (formerly Russian Orthodox Greek Catholic
    Church of America)
Pentecostal Assemblies of the World Inc.
Polish National Catholic Church of America
Presbyterian Church (U.S.A.)
Progressive National Baptist Convention
Religious Society of Friends (Conservative)
Religious Society of Friends (Unaffiliated Meetings)
Roman Catholic Church
Romanian Orthodox Episcopate of America
Serbian Orthodox Church in the U.S.A. and Canada
Seventh-day Adventist Church
Southern Baptist Convention
Syrian Orthodox Church of Antioch (Archdiocese of the United States and
    Canada)
Ukrainian Orthodox Church in America
Union of American Hebrew Congregations (Reform)
Union of Orthodox Jewish Congregations of America (Orthodox)
Unitarian Universalist Association
United Church of Christ (includes the former Evangelical and Reformed
    Church and most former Congregational Christian churches. Structure
    and terminology vary; check locally.)
United Methodist Church
United Synagogue of Conservative Judaism (Conservative)

HELP WITH QUESTIONS. A valuable source for names of denominations,
church statistics and histories, headquarters addresses, and telephone
numbers is the *Yearbook of American and Canadian Churches,* which
is published by the National Council of Churches, 475 Riverside Drive,
New York, NY 10115-0050. The telephone number for the yearbook is

(800) 672-1789. The telephone number of the council's public relations office is (212) 870-2227. See entries under individual church names.

department. Capitalize in the name of a primary agency of government and when part of the name of a company; lowercase alone and when part of the name of a subdivision of an agency or company: Department of Justice (Justice Department, the department); Sierra Vista Police Department (the Police Department, the department); the Departments of State and Agriculture, **but** the State and Agriculture departments, Rodney's Department Store, the clothing department. **Capitalize the names of other nations' comparable agencies:** Foreign Ministry (the ministry). **Lowercase departments of schools and colleges:** the Swarthmore history department, the English department. **Abbreviation,** *Dept.,* **is permitted in chart and table credits.** See CABINET DEPARTMENTS.

Depression, the. Capitalize in references to the period that began in 1929; lowercase otherwise. Also Great Depression.

des. See FRENCH NAMES and PARTICLES.

desalination means the same as desalinization, so use the shorter word.

descriptive clauses. See THAT, WHICH.

desert/dessert. As a verb, desert means to forsake or to leave. As a noun it is a dry, sandy place or a deserved reward or punishment, in the second case usually used in the plural (just deserts). Desserts are food.

(-)designate. Hyphenate: President-designate Katherine Tasoulis, the president-designate.

detective. Do not abbreviate. When it is a rank, capitalize it as a title before a name (police Detective Joseph Backhaus), but it is more often merely a job description, in which case it is lowercase: detective Sgt. Caitlin Kelley.

deutsche mark(s). German currency, commonly called mark.

devil. Capitalize when it means Satan; lowercase otherwise: The Devil made me do it. A devil made me do it. They say devils live there.

D

diacritics.
acute: éclat
grave: père
circumflex: château
cedilla: française
tilde: señorita
umlaut: Kurfürstendamm

Substituting *e* for an umlaut (*Duesseldorf* instead of *Düsseldorf,* for example) is a style followed primarily by publications that do not use diacritics. Since *U.S. News* uses umlauts, we do not substitute the *e.* However, some names actually do use *ae, oe,* and *ue* combinations, so be aware of the correct spelling. Correspondents should avoid spelling ä as *ae,* and so on, but indicate the umlaut in some way. Also, if a person really is named *Schoenhaus,* not *Schönhaus,* for example, the reporter should confirm that fact. Diacritics that are less familiar in the United States, such as Scandinavian, Polish, Czech, and Hungarian accents, are not used in *U.S. News.* In headlines, captions, and tables, except for capital letters and all-capital lines (as in photo credits and datelines), use diacritics as in body type.

dialect. See ACCENTS and SLANG, DIALECT, AND JARGON.

dice is plural; the singular is die.

dictionaries. Write names of dictionaries in italics. *U.S. News* uses:

1. *Webster's New World College Dictionary, Fourth Edition* (Macmillan). It is the first choice for spelling and definitions not included in this book.

2. *Webster's Third New International Dictionary* (Merriam-Webster, 1981). Use this as a backup for spelling, but for word usage it is not as reliable as the *New World.*

3. *Random House Unabridged Dictionary, Second Edition* (Random House) and *American Heritage Dictionary of the English Language, Fourth Edition* (Houghton Mifflin) are also backups for spelling.

4. *Merriam-Webster's Geographical Dictionary* (Merriam-Webster, 1997). Backup source for place names. See GEOGRAPHIC NAMES and SPELLING.

die-cast (adjective), die casting (noun)

digital audiotape. DAT is acceptable on second reference when the meaning is clear.

directions. See COMPASS DIRECTIONS.

disabled. Used as an adjective, this is preferred to "handicapped": disabled man, disabled person, disabled people, disabled veteran. Avoid using the word as a noun (*the disabled*), which emphasizes disability at the expense of individuality. See VICTIM.

disburse/disperse. Disburse is to pay out; disperse is to scatter.

diseases. In general, write them lowercase, except for any proper names they contain: measles, osteoarthritis, emphysema, atherosclerosis, Parkinson's disease, Hodgkin's disease. Recommended references: *Stedman's Medical Dictionary, Dorland's Illustrated Medical Dictionary, AMA Encyclopedia of Medicine, AMA Family Medical Guide, The Merck Manual.*

disk/disc. Use disk (disk-shaped object, disk brake, disk jockey, floppy disk, diskette, computer disk, disk drive, hard disk, compact disk, disk harrow, disk wheel, laserdisk, optical disk, videodisk), but for trademarked names, follow the company's spelling: Sony's MiniDisc.

disperse/disburse. Disperse is to scatter; disburse is to pay out.

district. Capitalize in names of congressional and legislative districts; lowercase alone except in reference to the District of Columbia: Fifth District, 23rd Congressional District (23rd District, the district).

District of Columbia (D.C., DC in addresses), the District

District of Columbia resident(s), Washingtonian, District resident, D.C. resident

divebomb (verb), dive bomber (noun)

division. Capitalize when used with a specific military number or designation; lowercase alone: 45th Division (the division), 2nd Airborne Division (the division). Lowercase when in the name of a subdivision of an agency or a company: antitrust division of the Justice Department, Chevrolet division of General Motors.

DMZ. Acceptable on second reference to demilitarized zone.

do. See PARTICLES.

doctor (Dr., Drs.). Abbreviate when used as a title before a name; spell out otherwise. By itself, *Dr.* is not particularly helpful to the reader, because of the wide range of disciplines that use the title. More useful is to specify the kind of doctorate a person holds (An advocate of weekly tests was Sara Matthews, a pathologist. Agronomist Carl Perkins agreed). Use *Dr.* as a title with a person's name in quoted matter; when needed for clarity, as when husbands and wives need to be distinguished from each other; and otherwise only when it is clear what kind of doctorate the person holds and the degree is earned (not honorary).

doctor of dental surgery (D.D.S.), a doctor of dental surgery degree

doctor of divinity (D.D.)

doctor of laws. See JURIS DOCTOR.

doctor of medicine (M.D.)

doctor of philosophy (Ph.D.)

doctrine. Capitalize in a recognized name; lowercase alone: Monroe Doctrine (the doctrine), Brezhnev Doctrine, preaching an isolationist doctrine.

dollar(s). Abbreviate, dol., only in charts, maps, and tables. Use the dollar sign with figures: $3 million.

do's and don'ts

dot com (noun), dot-com (adjective): Last week's big losers were the newer dot coms. Keating heads the latest dot-com sensation.

double genitive. In possessive expressions that use *of* and *'s*, the *'s*, although idiomatic, can often be used or dropped with no ill effect (a friend of the girl's, a friend of the girl), but in some cases the *'s* is required for understanding:
an opinion of the tutor's (an opinion held by the tutor)
an opinion of the tutor (someone else's opinion of the tutor)
a portrait of Chagall's (the portrait was created by Chagall)
a portrait of Chagall (Chagall is the subject of the portrait)

In some cases, a different preposition might work better: a portrait by Chagall. With pronouns, idiom invariably calls for the possessive form: a friend of mine, a book of yours.

double modifiers. See COMPOUND WORDS.

Dow Jones. Dow Jones industrial average (the Dow average). Indexes take a comma only when the number to the left of the decimal point is five or more digits: 3446.68; 18,889.

D

Down syndrome

downtrend

down under (Australia or New Zealand), but down-under policies

dpi. Acceptable for dots per inch when clear.

Dr. See DOCTOR.

drop in (verb), drop-in (noun)

drop off (verb), drop-off (noun)

drop out (verb), dropout (noun)

drugs. They include prescription and nonprescription pharmaceutical products and illegal substances such as heroin and marijuana, as well as beverage alcohol and tobacco products, so take care to use precise terms. For instance, don't write *He was addicted to drugs and alcohol* because alcohol is a drug and *drugs* is imprecise. Better: He was addicted to alcohol and barbiturates.

NAMES. In most cases, pharmaceutical drugs should be referred to by their generic names rather than by brand names: sulfisoxazole, not Gantrisin; tetracycline hydrochloride, not Achromycin. But if a point is being made about a particular brand, the brand name should be used. In some contexts, it may be desirable to use both names, as: Gantrisin, a brand of sulfisoxazole. Brands generally are capitalized, generic names lowercased.

Write generic names for illegal street drugs lowercase: crack, crank, heroin, ecstasy.

REFERENCES. Good sources for information are the *Physicians' Desk Reference* and *Drug Information for the Consumer,* published by *Consumer Reports* and the U.S. Pharmacopeial Convention.

drunk/drunken. As an adjective, drunk is usually used in the predicate (Austin was drunk), while drunken is used attributively (a drunken drummer). But drunk is also often used to distinguish a current state (drunk waiter) from a habitual one (drunken bum), and some states make a legal distinction between a drunk driver (one whose blood-alcohol level is above a certain limit) and a drunken driver (one who is merely inebriated).

dry goods (noun), dry-goods store (adjective)

du. See DU PONT, FRENCH NAMES, and PARTICLES.

Dubya. Acceptable, when clear, for casual references to George W. Bush, but avoid in serious news articles, except when quoting someone. When a written quote uses "W" as a nickname for Bush, write it without a period.

due. Correct when *due* modifies a noun: rain due to a cold front or autos due this fall. Incorrect when there is no modified noun, as in *She went due to an emergency.* In that case, use *because of* instead.

duke. See NOBILITY.

Du Pont. This name takes various forms in different branches of the family. The company's full name is E. I. du Pont de Nemours & Co., but it's the DuPont Co. or DuPont (no space between *Du* and *Pont*). See the electronic NAMES list.

duty-free. She mailed the duty-free gifts, but These goods moved duty free.

DVD is acceptable on first reference to digital video disk.

executive order

earl. See NOBILITY.

earth. Lowercase except when personified or when referring to the planet: rich, dark earth; down to earth; returning to Earth; Can Earth survive?; "I am the daughter of Earth and Water"; traveling from Mars to Earth; traveling from Earth to the moon; They built the largest telescope on Earth.

east, eastern. See COMPASS DIRECTIONS.

East Room (of the White House)

easy money (noun), easy-money (adjective)

ecology is a branch of biology. Do not use it as a synonym for ecosystem or environment.

ECU(s). Acceptable on second reference to European currency unit(s).

editors' notes. See BYLINES.

EDT. See TIME ZONES.

effect. As a verb, effect means to bring about a result: The movers effected a speedy transition; as a noun, it means a result: The music had a soothing effect on everyone. As a verb, affect means to influence or to make a pretense of: How did she affect the outcome? He affected a nonplused attitude. Affect is used as a noun in psychology, where it means an emotion attached to an idea, object, etc.

-elect. President-elect Lauch (the president-elect).

Election Day

Electoral College

electric/electronic/electronics. Electric light bulbs and electric motors are run by electricity. Electronic pianos and electronic rectifiers are operated by a flow of electrons controlled by tubes or transistors. Electronics is a branch of physics: electronics industry.

ellipsis points. Use an ellipsis (three points, separated by thin spaces so the points won't be divided by a line break) to indicate deletions in quotes, textual matter, and documents. Put a regular space before and after the ellipsis (The law states: "He shall be hanged . . . till dead."). Use a period and three points when the deletion occurs after the end of a sentence ("That was the end of the case. . . . Sentencing came on Tuesday."). If you break off a sentence before the end, put a space before the period, then an ellipsis ("That was the end . . . . Sentencing came on Tuesday."). Retain the original punctuation before or after a deletion only if necessary to the sense of the sentence:

"To sharpen the knife, you must use a stone."
"To sharpen the knife . . . use a stone."
"Observe these herbs: thyme, rosemary, and oregano."
"Observe these herbs: . . . rosemary and oregano."

End quotes that trail off with an ellipsis: "I might run," Matthews said, "if . . . ." See DASH.

E-mail addresses. When appropriate, put addresses in italics. Avoid breaking an E-mail address over a line. If that is not practical, delete the line-break hyphen and force the line break by hitting shift/enter. If a break occurs at a period, put the period on the next line.

embassy. Capitalize in a name; lowercase alone: the Canadian Embassy (the embassy), the French and Canadian embassies.

emigrate. People emigrate *from* and immigrate *to:* Moulier emigrated from France. He immigrated to the United States.

employee

encyclopedias. Set names italic. See BOOK TITLES.

en dash. Longer than a hyphen, shorter than the standard dash (em dash), an en dash is used as a minus sign and between inclusive numbers, and it may be substituted for a hyphen to promote clarity: white-collar–blue-collar contrast, first-come–first-served policy. To get an en dash, hit shift and the + key. See DASH.

engine. Generally, use engine for devices that develop their own power, motor for devices powered by external means: airplane engine, electric motor, a car engine's starter motor.

-engine. four-engine plane

en route

ensure. To make sure or make safe. Use *insure* with regard to insurance. Use *assure* when the meaning is "to promise confidently."

Episcopal Church. On subsequent reference, the church. Members are Episcopalians. The adjective is Episcopal. The Rev. Andrew Tucker, deacon of St. Dunstan's Episcopal Church (the deacon). Some priests prefer to be addressed as *Father* or *Mother*. The Rev. Janice Parker, rector of All Souls' Episcopal Church (Mother Parker, Parker, the minister, a minister); Suffragan Bishop Donald Schurick of Virginia, or of the Diocese of Virginia (Bishop Schurick, the bishop); Canon Elise Andrews (Canon Andrews, the canon). Presiding Bishop James Grier of the Episcopal Church (Presiding Bishop Grier, Bishop Grier, the presiding bishop, the bishop); the Very Rev. Catherine Stevens, dean of Birmingham Cathedral (Dean Stevens, the dean).

epithets. Do not use derogatory terms for racial, national, religious, sectional, or ethnic groups or demeaning language related to color, creed, sex, age, marital status, national origin, personal appearance, political affiliation, or mental or physical disability, except in quotations and then only when essential to a story. See FAIRNESS and GENDER BIAS.

epoch. Capitalize historical designations: Pleistocene Epoch. Capitalize Ice Age when referring to the Pleistocene Epoch; lowercase otherwise: Ice Age humans, but the latest ice age. See AGES AND ERAS.

eras. See AGES AND ERAS.

EST. See TIME ZONES.

establishment. Lowercase, it often appears with a modifier (the recording-industry establishment) and refers to an organization or a grouping of tangentially related interests. Capitalized, as in the Establishment, it should be used sparingly and by itself to refer to an inner group that holds controlling power.

ethics committee. Informal name for the House Committee on Standards of Official Conduct.

ethnic identification. Do not use unless it is clearly relevant to a story.

Eucharist. See SACRAMENTS.

Euro( ). Hyphenate when followed by capitalization; otherwise make solid: Euro-Communist, Eurodollar.

euro(s). European currency.

European Union (EU). See electronic NAMES list.

even money (noun), even-money (adjective)

E

ever. Do not hyphenate in constructions like ever increasing income.

every day (adverb): Katherine goes nearly every day; everyday (adjective): It was just an everyday trip.

ex. When it means former, use a hyphen: ex-president.

exact words. Define your terms. What is "upper class"? What is "middle class"? Is the next class down "lower class"? Do you mean "middle income"? In the search for exact terms, it is helpful to avoid, when possible, words that are used imprecisely: At Columbus, Ohio, a new facility for the Nessel Co. is nearing completion. What is it? A bathroom? A 3-acre factory? In Denver, a new library is underway. Is someone campaigning for a new library? Are plans being drawn for one? Has ground been broken? Is work nearly complete on it? Is the library already in operation? Many villages have closed their local jails. Hundreds? More than 100? Ten?

excess-profits tax

exclamation point. Use very sparingly. It goes inside quotation marks when part of a quotation, outside otherwise.

execute, execution. These involve legal killing. Do not use for, say, gangland or guerrilla slayings carried out in the manner of an official killing. In those cases, use an expression like execution-style killing.

Executive Office (of the president of the United States)

executive order. Capitalize when part of a name; lowercase otherwise: The president issued Executive Order 107. The president issued an executive order.

exhibit. Capitalize with a letter or a number: Exhibit A, Exhibit 13 (the exhibit).

exhibitions, titles of. Set roman with quotation marks: "Jean Ingres in Paradise."

expert. Avoid overuse or misuse. Not everyone who pontificates on an issue is an expert. Specialist is often a more objective alternative.

Export-Import Bank. Ex-Im Bank is acceptable on second reference.

extra( ). Meaning outside or beyond, it usually combines solid except before a capitalization or an *a:* extramarital, extraordinary, but extra-base hit. Meaning "especially," it is a separate word: extra expensive.

eye to eye. They saw eye to eye, an eye-to-eye confrontation. Use *eyeball* similarly.

flaunt/flout

facade

face-lift

face to face. They stood face to face, a face-to-face standoff.

fact-finder

fact-finding (noun and adjective)

Fahrenheit. To convert from Celsius, multiply by 1.8, then add 32. See
TEMPERATURE.

fairness. A good general approach is to apply the golden rule: Imagine
yourself as the object of any characterizations or aspersions in your story,
and treat the individuals involved as you would wish to be treated. Among
the many considerations that writers, supervising editors, and copy editors should bring to bear on this subject are the following:

SENSITIVE TOPICS. Examples include criminal charges, lawsuits, and
other accusations; personal matters, such as sexual behavior and sexual orientation; and any situation involving children.

FACTUAL CORRECTNESS is a primary consideration. Quoting a person or
publication does not excuse us for a mistake of fact or judgment.

UP-TO-DATE INFORMATION IS ESSENTIAL. It is important, where feasible, that we keep current and avoid working just from old material. A
judge's opinion in a court proceeding, for example, may be subject to further proceedings, appeals, or other changes.

ALL SIDES ARE IMPORTANT. If a person is accused in any manner or
the person's position is attacked, every effort must be made to present the
individual's reply. If our sources have not or will not provide a response
to us, newspaper articles, court documents, or other sources may show
that the individual has replied to the accusation or attack in another
forum. If a reference by a person being interviewed may be harmful to another person, efforts should be made to contact the other person.

SUITABLE WORDS are a matter for careful choice and examination, to
avoid any implication of guilt when guilt has not been proved in court.
"Arrested for theft," for example, can be read as implying guilt in some
contexts. "Arrested on a charge of theft" is a better way to say it if that
really is the charge—and we must make certain it is an official charge. *The
culprits* and similar phrases can, depending on the context, raise issues

of fairness. First, such phrases lump together several individuals, some of whom may suffer by association. Second, they may indicate guilt when no guilt has been proved.

CAPTION WRITING presents another concern. Crowd scenes in which people can be identified are often troublesome. For instance, if a photograph illustrates a crime or disorder, our description must be tailored to avoid naming as perpetrators any persons who in fact might be innocent bystanders. Another example is the use of a child's photograph in a story about classes for developmentally disabled children; in certain circumstances, it may be useful to check with the photographer or photography editor to confirm that the child is in fact developmentally disabled.

LEGAL ADVICE IS IMPORTANT. While the foregoing are examples of the concerns to consider when thinking about fairness, our reporting, writing, and editing may raise legal issues on which the advice of counsel would be helpful. When in doubt, do not hesitate to seek that advice. See EPITHETS, GENDER BIAS, and PHYSICAL APPEARANCE.

fall or autumn

faraway, but You are far away.

Farm Belt

far-off, but The date is far off.

farther/further. Farther is concerned with physical distances (running farther); further is concerned with abstract relationships of degree or quantity. It also means more or additional (further considerations).

Far West. See POLITICAL REGIONS.

faze/phase. Faze is to disturb or disconcert. As a noun, phase is a stage; as a verb, it means to introduce in stages.

FBI is acceptable on first reference when the meaning is clear.

February. See DATES and MONTHS.

federal. Capitalize in a name; lowercase otherwise: Federal Communications Commission, federal Department of Labor, federal employees, federal budget, federal Judge Susan Black.

Federal Register. Italicize. See TITLES OF WORKS.

Federal Reserve Board, Federal Reserve, the Fed (on second reference)

fellow. Lowercase: a university fellow, a Nieman fellow, the fellowship, but a Nieman Fellowship.

fellow man. See GENDER BIAS.

female/woman. In general, when an adjective is called for in referring to a woman, use *female;* when a noun is called for, use *woman.*

fewer measures numbers, not volume: fewer birds, less corn. When writing about ratios and percentages, use *fewer* when dealing with things that can be counted (except when less than 1), *less* when dealing with quantity: fewer than 3 in 10 editors attend seminars; less than 1 nurse in 6 lives nearby; fewer than 50 percent of the company's employees are graduates, less than 50 percent of the company's workforce is covered.

figure. Capitalize with a number or a letter: Figure IV, Figure B, the figure.

figures. See NUMBERS.

firearms are weapons, usually hand-held, whose projectiles are expelled by an explosive charge. (Air guns, which use compressed air to shoot BBs or pellets, are not firearms.)

ASSAULT RIFLE, ASSAULT WEAPON. Avoid the terms, but if you must use them, make clear what kind you are writing about because definitions vary. In military parlance, an assault weapon is a compact rifle, firing intermediate-size ammunition, that can be fired *automatically.* But federal legislation includes in its definition of assault weapon various *semiautomatic* rifles and pistols that resemble their automatic-firing counterparts. When the weapon in question does not fall under the military definition, make clear that you are writing about semiautomatic weapons and qualify the terms with quotation marks (semiautomatic "assault pistol") or use such phrases as assault-type rifle, assault-style rifle, or so-called assault rifle.

AUTOMATIC. Any firearm that continues to fire as long as the trigger is held or until the ammunition is exhausted.

SEMIAUTOMATIC. Any firearm that fires, ejects the casing, and reloads each time the trigger is pulled.

SELECT FIRE. Characteristic that allows a weapon to be fired either semi-automatically, automatically, or in bursts (when a certain number of rounds are fired each time the trigger is pulled).

BULLET. Projectile expelled by small arms. If you use the term *armor-piercing bullet,* make clear what kind of armor the bullet in question can penetrate. *Cop-killer bullet* is an imprecise and inflammatory term that should be avoided.

CALIBER. The measure, in hundredths of an inch or millimeters, of a bullet's nominal diameter: .45-caliber revolver, 9-mm pistol, .22-caliber rifle, .50-caliber machine gun, .357-caliber Magnum, .30-30 rifle (.30 caliber, 30 grains of powder in cartridge), .30-06 rifle (.30 caliber, introduced in 1906).

CARBINE. A short, lightweight rifle, usually having a barrel length of less than 20 inches: M-1 carbine.

CARTRIDGE. It consists of a bullet, primer, propellant, and cartridge case (casing). Also called a round of ammunition.

CLIP. A detachable device that stores ammunition and feeds it into a gun.

GAUGE. The bore size of a shotgun. The smaller the gauge, the bigger the shotgun: 12-gauge shotgun, a 10-gauge. (The .410, which actually refers to the caliber, is an exception and is designated .410 bore.)

HANDGUN. A firearm designed to be held and fired using one hand, although in practice it is often fired using two hands for stability.

LONG GUN. A small-arm weapon designed to be fired from the shoulder. It includes rifles and shotguns.

MACHINE GUN. An automatic-firing weapon designed for military or paramilitary use. Subcategories are: MACHINE PISTOL. It fires pistol ammunition and can be held and operated with one hand. SUBMACHINE GUN. A lightweight, short-barreled, hand-carried weapon exemplified by the Thompson submachine gun. LIGHT MACHINE GUN. It fires rifle ammunition and is often mounted on a bipod and may require two operators. MEDIUM MACHINE GUN. It fires rifle ammunition and is usually mounted on a tripod and operated by a crew of three or more. HEAVY MACHINE GUN. It fires ammunition larger than standard rifle cartridges.

MAGAZINE. A device that stores ammunition and feeds it into a gun. Detachable box-type magazines are usually called clips.

MAGNUM. Trademark for a high-powered cartridge: .357-caliber Magnum. It is also used to describe guns that fire such ammunition.

PISTOL. Technically, a handgun whose barrel is integral with the ammunition chamber; however, in common usage it can refer to any handgun, including revolvers.

REVOLVER. A handgun whose ammunition is held in a cylinder that rotates.

RIFLE. A long gun with a rifled (spirally grooved) bore, which imparts a spin to the bullet to improve stability and accuracy.

RIFLED SLUG. A lead projectile with grooves, designed to be fired from a shotgun.

SAWED-OFF SHOTGUN/SAWED-OFF RIFLE. A shotgun with a barrel shorter than 18 inches, a rifle with a barrel shorter than 16 inches, or an overall length for either of less than 26 inches.

SHOT. Pellets that make up the projectile in a shotgun.

SHOTGUN. A long gun with a smooth bore that fires pellets and rifled slugs.

SMALL ARMS. Hand-held firearms with a caliber of .50 or less.

fire resistance, fire-resistant curtain, but the curtain was fire resistant.

first class (noun and adverb), first-class (adjective)

first come, first served; first-come–first-served policy

first family, first lady, first cat, etc.

firsthand. firsthand information; They got the information firsthand, but at first hand.

first in, first out; first-in–first-out system

first person. See WE.

flair/flare. Flair is an ability or an artistic style; flare is a signal device or to flame or to curve outward.

flaunt/flout. Flaunt is to show off; flout is to show contempt for.

fleet. Capitalize in a name; lowercase alone: 6th Fleet, Atlantic Fleet, the U.S. fleet (the fleet).

flextime

flier for pamphlets, pilots, and passengers

flight. Capitalize with a number; lowercase alone: US Airways Flight 171, Flight 171 (the flight).

Florida (Fla., FL in addresses)

Floridian

flout. See FLAUNT/FLOUT.

fly swatter

f.o.b. Acceptable on first reference to free on board when the meaning is clear.

( )fold. twofold, threefold, 12-fold, 50-fold. When 10 grows twofold, it becomes 20; when 10 grows fourfold, it becomes 40.

foot, feet. Abbreviate, ft., only in charts, maps, and tables.

foot-dragging

footnotes. Use footnote symbols in this sequence: *, †, **, ‡. Notes and footnotes end with periods, even when no sentence is formed. Source lines do not. See CHARTS AND TABLES.

forbear/forebear. Forbear is to refrain; forebear is an ancestor.

fore( ). Write solid except before capitalization or an *e*.

forego/forgo. Forego is to precede (a foregone conclusion); forgo is to relinquish or do without (Let's forgo dessert).

foreign. When referring to the world at large, be sensitive that *international* may be preferable to *foreign,* which often implies antipathy or antagonism.

foreign currencies. See CURRENCIES.

foreign names. See ARABIC NAMES, BRAZILIAN NAMES, CHINESE NAMES, FRENCH NAMES, GERMAN NAMES, PARTICLES, PORTUGUESE NAMES, RUSSIAN NAMES, SPANISH-LANGUAGE NAMES, and the electronic NAMES and PLACES lists.

foreign officials, titles of. See TITLES OF PERSONS.

Foreign Service

foreign words. Italicize them when they are designated as such in the dictionary. If you use a word not in the dictionary but known to you as foreign, italicize it, too, unless it is a proper noun. See GERMAN COMMON NOUNS and ITALICS.

foreword/forward. A foreword is an introductory section in a book, usually written by someone other than the author; forward means toward the front or an offensive player in various sports.

forgo. See FOREGO/FORGO.

form. Capitalize with a number or a letter: Form 1040, Form B (the form).

Fort. Do not abbreviate except in charts, maps, and tables.

fortuitous/fortunate. Use fortuitous when you mean "accidental." Use fortunate when you mean "favorable" or "advantageous."

***Fortune* 500.** Italicize *Fortune*.

forward. See FOREWORD/FORWARD.

foundation. Capitalize in a name; lowercase alone: the John D. and Catherine T. MacArthur Foundation (the MacArthur Foundation, the foundation).

Founding Fathers. Capitalize only when referring to Alexander Hamilton et al.

401(k), 401(k)'s

fractions. Spell out and hyphenate when a fraction is used as an adjective and not part of a larger figure: It was two-thirds gone. Do not hyphenate when used as a noun: He buried one third of the total. When the denominator itself is hyphenated, drop the hyphen between the numerator and the denominator: four twenty-fifths. When a fraction is added to a number, use figures for the entire number: $2^1/_2$ days. See ORDINAL NUMBERS.

(-)free. duty-free goods; these goods moved duty free; tax-free bonds; These bonds are tax free.

free world. Don't use except in quotes. Use a specific geographical term or "non-Communist world," if that is what is meant.

freight carloadings

french doors, french dressing, french-fried onion rings, french fries, french leave

French names. Follow the individual's preference on spelling and capitalization of personal names. *La, Le, Les* are usually capitalized: Maurice de La Gorce (the La Gorce story, La Gorce). *Des* and *Du* are usually capitalized if they occur at the start of a surname: Pierre Du Pré (Du Pré), Armand Dupré (Dupré). But watch out for double surnames. They raise questions not only of capitalization but of recognition; you have to be sure you do not mistake the first half of a double surname for a given, or first, name. Interior particles are likely to be lowercase: Bernard Reynold du Chaffaut (Reynold du Chaffaut). The contractions *d'* and *de* are usually lowercase. See PARTICLES.

Friends, Religious Society of. Shorten to the Society of Friends on subsequent mention or to Friends in such subsequent references as the Friends' attitude toward war. The Friends also may be called Quakers. The Society of Friends operates through five main groups: Friends General Conference, Friends United Meeting, Evangelical Friends International—North America Region, Religious Society of Friends (Conservative), and Religious Society of Friends (Unaffiliated Meetings). There are also some smaller unaffiliated groups. A local congregation is often formally known as a monthly meeting, capitalized when part of a name: Oak Grove Monthly Meeting of Friends. Most congregations have a less formal name (the geographic or "given" name), plus "Friends Meeting" or "Friends Church." Some monthly meetings have no clergy; others have leaders called pastors or executive secretaries: John P. Piluk, pastor of Oak Grove Friends Meeting. Friends pastors in North America almost never use titles such as "Reverend," although practices vary in the rest of the world. Monthly meetings are organized into quarterly or half-yearly meetings, and these are grouped into yearly meetings, which correspond to dioceses in some other denominations. These terms are capitalized when used in names. Quarterly or half-yearly meetings and yearly meetings are run by officials with the title of clerk: Frank Konkus, clerk of the Center City Yearly Meeting. Yearly meetings in the Society of Friends maintain contact with each other through the five main groups mentioned above and through the Friends World Committee for Consultation, to which almost all send delegates or observers.

front line (noun), front-line (adjective)

full-time. They have full-time jobs. They are working full time.

fuse

gallon(s). Abbreviate, gal., only in charts, maps, and tables.

game, Game 3, but the third game

gantlet/gauntlet. A gantlet is a section of overlapping railroad track or a punishment involving running between rows of hitters; a gauntlet is a glove. *To throw down the gauntlet* is to issue a challenge.

GAO. Acceptable on second reference to General Accounting Office.

GATT. Acceptable on second reference to General Agreement on Tariffs and Trade, which was superseded in 1995 by the World Trade Organization.

gay (noun and adjective). Acceptable for references to male and female homosexuals. See HOMOSEXUAL.

GDP. Acceptable on second reference to gross domestic product.

GED. Acceptable for general equivalency diploma when the meaning is clear.

Gen. Gen. Mason Cunnion (General Cunnion, the general). See MILITARY TITLES.

gender bias. Consider alternatives to language that emphasizes a person's sex or that implies certain occupations are in the exclusive domain of men or women, that betrays surprise at finding, for example, a woman in a professional or executive position or a man in a nursing or nurturing field. Avoid nouns, such as poetess, whose very existence often implies that the masculine form is the standard and the feminine form is exceptional.

LIMITING TERMS THAT MAY BE OFFENSIVE	POSSIBLE ALTERNATIVES
anchorman, anchorwoman	anchor
businessman, businesswoman	businessperson, business executive
businessmen	businesspersons, business people
career woman	(name the job or profession)
chairman	chair, chairperson, presiding officer
coed (noun)	student
comedienne	comedian
congressman	member of Congress, representative
councilman	council member
countryman	compatriot
craftsman	craftsperson, artisan

LIMITING TERMS THAT MAY BE OFFENSIVE	POSSIBLE ALTERNATIVES
eight-man board	eight-member board, eight-person board
female lawyer	lawyer
fireman	firefighter
fisherman	fisher, angler
foreman	supervisor
garbage man	garbage collector
housewife	homemaker
layman	layperson
mailman	letter carrier, postal worker
male nurse, model	nurse, model
man and wife	husband and wife
patrolman, policeman	police officer
poetess	poet
salesman	salesperson
sculptress	sculptor
stewardess	flight attendant, steward

Such dictionary-sanctioned words as *chairperson* and *spokesperson* are acceptable, but do not coin *-person* words. Consider alternatives to language that identifies the male as the archetype of the human race. Substitutions need not always be made when the cure would be worse than the disease.

WORDS OBJECTED TO	POSSIBLE SUBSTITUTES
fellow man	fellow human, fellow citizen
man, mankind	humankind, humanity, the human race, people
manpower	staff, personnel, human resources, workforce
man's accomplishments	human accomplishments
man's spirit	the human spirit
workingman	worker, wage earner
the man for the job	the person for the job
man-made	artificial, synthetic, machine made, handmade
the common man	ordinary people
one man, one vote	one person, one vote

Avoid language that stereotypes women as sex objects, cute, scatterbrained, timorous, shrewish, etc., and men as chauvinistic, loutish, insensitive, rude, etc. Additional alternatives to objectionable language are available in *The Handbook of Nonsexist Writing* by Casey Miller and Kate Swift (Harper & Row, 1988). See EPITHETS, FAIRNESS, HE/SHE, and MAN.

general. Capitalize before a name; lowercase otherwise. Abbreviate before a full name; spell out otherwise: Gen. Les Hall (General Hall, the general). See MILITARY TITLES.

General Assembly. Capitalize in the name of a state or national governing body and in references to the United Nations body: the U.N. General Assembly (the General Assembly, the Assembly), the Arkansas General Assembly (the General Assembly, the Assembly).

generation X, X-er, gen X-ers

Geneva Conventions, the conventions. There are four, dated 1864, 1907, 1929, and 1949. Two additional protocols were adopted in 1977.

genie(s). Wish granters.

genus and species. In technical contexts, capitalize the genus name, lowercase the species name, and italicize both: *Homo sapiens, Canis lupus.* On second reference, the genus name may be abbreviated: *C. lupus.* Members of classifications broader than genus (kingdom, phylum, class, order, and family) are capitalized and roman: Mammalia. English derivatives and nontechnical uses sanctioned by the dictionaries may be set roman, lowercase: amoebas, homo sapiens. See INFECTIOUS ORGANISMS.

geographic names. For spelling and capitalization, use these references in the following order:

1. This stylebook, including the electronic PLACES list.
2. *National Five-digit ZIP Code & Post Office Directory* (National Information Data Center).
3. *Webster's New World College Dictionary, Fourth Edition* (Macmillan, 1999).
4. *Merriam-Webster's Geographical Dictionary* (Merriam-Webster, 1997).
5. *National Geographic Atlas of the World.* (When a name in this atlas is followed by one with a different spelling in parentheses, *U.S. News* generally uses the one in parentheses; for example, Lisbon instead of *Lisboa.*)
6. *Columbia Lippincott Gazetteer of the World.*

POSSESSIVE APOSTROPHES. Some implied-possessive place names are spelled with an apostrophe (Martha's Vineyard, Prince George's County), but most are not (Pikes Peak, Harpers Ferry, Nags Head). For such place names that have no primary-source spelling and are not listed in the above references, use *s* without an apostrophe (Fells Point). See NATIONS AND REGIONS and the electronic PLACES list.

geographic terms. Capitalize places, real or imaginary, with special names: Badlands, Southern Highlands, Death Valley, Big Bend, Everglades, Black Hills, Rockies, Smokies, Black Forest, Twin Cities, Border States, the Downs, the Promised Land, Lake District (England). See CENTRAL, COMPASS DIRECTIONS, individual entries, such as ISLAND(S), RIVER, etc., and the electronic PLACES list.

Georgia (Ga., GA in addresses)

Georgian

German common nouns. If they are used as foreign words, italicize them, lowercase. If the dictionary indicates they are anglicized, set them roman, lowercase.

German names. Use the diphthongs *ae, ie, oe,* or *ue* only if you know that to be the way the individual's name is spelled; if the name uses an umlaut, use the umlaut; don't substitute the extra *e:* Wolfgang von Goethe (that's the way it's spelled), Erich Spätmann (if he spells it that way; not *Spaetmann*).

Germany. When referring to the formerly separate nations and cities, use East Germany, West Germany, East Berlin, and West Berlin. When referring to sections of the unified nation, use eastern Germany, western Germany, east Berlin, and west Berlin. Capitalize East and West when standing alone and referring to the former nations as well as to the post-unification sections: Development in the East has not reached projections made in 1990.

gerunds. See APOSTROPHE.

ghetto(s). Avoid overuse when referring to an area where poor people or minorities live. Section, area, district, and slum (if that's what is meant) often are better alternatives.

GI(s). Lowercase *s* even in all-caps headlines.

gibe/jibe. Gibe is to jeer or taunt; jibe is to be in agreement or to shift sails.

GI Bill. (An exception to the general rule on *bill*.) See BILL.

gigabyte. 1 gigabyte, 4 gigabytes, a 12-gigabyte hard drive. GB and gigs are acceptable on second reference when the meaning is clear: 1GB, 4GB, 4 gigs.

girl. Do not use for women 18 and older.

glossary

BODY TYPE is the standard type used in the text of an article, as opposed to display type (headlines, etc.). In *U.S. News,* body type is usually 9 points.

CHATTER is the chart and table type that elaborates on the headline.

CREDITS are used to indicate who contributed a particular photograph, illustration, etc.

"DOWN" STYLE is the tendency of a publication to lowercase words that could be either capped or lowercased (for example, lowercasing *administration* when it refers to a specific government). With regard to headlines, capitalization under "down" style is generally limited to words that begin a sentence, proper nouns, initialisms, and titles used before a name. In "up" style headlines, initial letters in all words are capitalized except the articles *a, an,* and *the;* the conjunctions *and, but, or, as,* and *if;* prepositions of three letters or fewer; and the second element of "permanent" compound words. Adverbs that form an integral part of a verb are also capped.

DECK is a headline that is in smaller type than the main headline and comes just after it.

ELECTRONIC NAMES AND PLACES LISTS. They contain names of people, geographical locations, and other proper nouns in the news. They are available in the TeamBase stylebook-usn queue.

EM DASH is the standard dash, so called because it is usually about as long as a capital M. Get it by hitting ctrl/shift +.

EN DASH is longer than a hyphen and shorter than a regular dash (the em dash) and is used as a minus sign, between inclusive numbers, and in such constructions as *first-in–first-out system.* Get it by hitting shift +.

FLUSH LEFT (ENTER) aligns type along a left-hand margin.

FORCED JUSTIFICATION (shift ENTER) ends a line of type and justifies it (adding enough space between words to make the line fill the width of its column).

KICKER is the last paragraph in an article.

NUT GRAF. The paragraph that contains an article's essence, core, or theme.

PERMANENT COMPOUND WORDS are those found in the dictionary (self-esteem) as opposed to newly created compounds (tough-love therapy).

POINT means the same as period.

PRECEDE. Larger than standard body type, smaller than headline type, a precede is used as an introduction to a major article.

PULLOUT. A device that uses display type to repeat information, often a quote, taken from an article. Also called "liftout" and "pullquote."

RUBRIC. A headline identifying a section or a subject, like News You Can Use, Electronics.

RUNNING FOOT, also called a footline, is the type at the bottom of a page giving the issue date and the name of the publication. It often also includes the folio (page number).

"SET ROMAN" means to put the indicated material in roman type.

SIDEBAR. A short article, often boxed, that is related to or elaborates on a main article.

SIDEHEAD is bold body type that takes up less than a full line of type and is usually followed by a period, then integrated with regular body type.

SKYLINE. A cover headline that goes above the nameplate. Also called a roofline.

SLUG. The unique name given to a file, such as an article, caption, or sidebar, that will be published.

SMALL CAPS. Designed to reduce the visual jumble in body type created by initialisms, small-cap type is capitalized in form but smaller in size than standard capitals (full caps). They are also used in datelines and in the first line of letters to the editor.

"SOLID" means to make the combination in question one word, unhyphenated (*Eurodollar*).

SUBHEAD. Bold body type that occupies a line by itself.

THIN SPACE is used to regularize spacing and prevent bad line breaks, as between ellipsis points and between quotation marks and subquotation marks. It is created with ctrl/shift and the spacebar.

TOP EDITOR is the highest-ranking editor responsible for a particular article.

GM. Acceptable on first reference to General Motors when the context makes its meaning clear.

GMT. Acceptable for Greenwich Mean Time when clear.

GNP. Acceptable on second reference to gross national product.

God. See DEITY.

( )goer. Combines solid except when an awkward combination would result: operagoer, Mardi Gras goer, strawberry-festival-goer.

goodbye

Good Friday

goodwill

GOP. Acceptable for Republican Party after first reference.

gorillas/guerrillas. Gorillas are animals; guerrillas are fighters.

got/gotten. They often can be used interchangeably, but *got* is generally preferred when it means "being in possession of" (I have got the money) and *gotten* when it means "have obtained" (I have gotten plenty of money). Using more-precise verbs (or just dropping *got*) can often do a better job: I have the money. I received the money.

government. Lowercase except in a name: the U.S. government, the federal government, the Italian government, Government Employees Insurance Co., Government Printing Office.

governor. Capitalize and abbreviate before a full name. Spell out with last name only. Lowercase alone: Gov. William Donald Schaefer (Governor Schaefer, the governor). But spell out and lowercase when used with persons other than governmental chief executives: Federal Reserve governor Janet Yellen.

grade. first-grade pupil, grade seven, grades 10 to 12, 10th-grade student, low-grade uranium, grade A eggs.

grader. first grader, 10th grader.

grades. Capitalize, no quotes: She got an A minus. Two B's were enough. Plus and minus signs are acceptable when the meaning is clear: Ashley received an A+ on her term paper.

graduate. She graduated from Trinity is preferred. She was graduated from Trinity is acceptable. Do not write *She graduated Trinity* or *She graduated college.*

gram(s). Spell out on first reference. Abbreviation, g, is acceptable on second reference and in charts and tables.

gray

greater than/as great as. They don't mean the same thing. If Andy makes $50,000 a year and Amy makes $200,000, Amy's salary is four times *as great as* Andy's and three times *greater than* Andy's. To avoid ambiguity, use the former construction. The same kind of problem exists with "times more" (use "times as many"), "times higher" (use "as high as"), and "times larger" (use "as large as"). *Times smaller* is mathematically impossible; use a percent or fraction instead.

great-grandfather, great-great-grandfather, great-great-great-grandmother, six greats-grandmother (the mother of a person's great-great-great-great-great-grandmother)

grounds. Use the plural when it means basis or foundation.

groundswell

group. Capitalize in a name or with a letter or a number: the Cotter Advertising Group, Group W, Group A2, the Group of Eight industrialized nations (G-8).

groups, names of

actors	troupe	lions	pride
ants	colony	monkeys (large group)	troop
bees	swarm	monkeys (small group)	gang
birds	flight	pigs	drove
chickens	flock	porpoises	school
fish	school	quails	bevy, covy
geese	flock, gaggle	rabbits	warren
goats	herd	sheep	flock, herd

hens	flock	whales	pod
horses	team	witches	coven
hounds	pack	wolves	pack
insects	swarm		

For more, see *An Exaltation of Larks* by James Lipton (Penguin, 1993).

guarantee. Use *Guaranty* only in names that spell it that way.

Guard. See NATIONAL GUARD.

guerrillas/gorillas. Guerrillas are fighters; gorillas are animals.

gulf. Capitalize when part of a name and when referring to the Gulf of Mexico; lowercase otherwise: Gulf of Suez (the gulf), Persian Gulf (Gulf War, gulf states), Gulf of Mexico (the Gulf, Gulf States—meaning Alabama, Florida, Louisiana, Mississippi, and Texas).

guns. See FIREARMS.

gyp. Use only in quotations and then only when essential to a story. Acceptable alternatives include *fraud, cheat, con, scam,* and *swindle.*

Gypsy. Capitalize references to Romany people: Gypsies were erroneously thought to have come from Egypt; Charles VI had all Gypsy men put to death. Lowercase otherwise: the gypsy in me, a gypsy violin, gypsy moth. Find and use alternatives to expressions that imply denigration: *gypsy cab* (unlicensed cab), *gypsy plumber* (nonunion plumber).

hell

Hades, but lowercase hell.

hail/hale. hail (an ice pellet; to greet, call out, name by way of tribute); hail from (to come from); hale (healthy, to pull forcibly). Hail fell while they hailed her as victor; she hailed a taxi; he hailed from Cedar City; hale and hearty at 87; she was haled into court.

half(-). Follow the dictionary on whether to make combinations two words, solid, or hyphenated (half dollar, halfback, half-hour, halftime). Combinations not in the dictionary are generally two words when used as a noun (half century, half dozen, half mile), hyphenated when used as an adjective (half-century, half-dozen, half-mile).

hand drill (noun), hand-drill (adjective and verb)

(-)handed. Hyphenate made-up combinations: awkward-handed.

hand-held (noun and adjective)

handicap. Don't use to mean disability. A person with a disability who uses a wheelchair, for instance, is handicapped by a stairway. The person is disabled; the stairway is the handicap. See DISABLED and VICTIM.

handyman, but He is a handy man in a fight.

hanged, hung. For executions, lynchings, and suicides, use hanged; for everything else, use hung.

Hanukkah

hard-pressed. It is a hard-pressed species, but the species is hard pressed.

Hawaii (HI in addresses; otherwise do not abbreviate)

Hawaiian

headlines. Figures may be used in headlines for numbers of any size, but be consistent within a headline: 3 VISITS YIELD 13 SALES. Use single quotes in headlines and decks, double quotes in precedes and sideheads. Use special, shorter em dashes (–, made by hitting ctrl/shift/alt/+) in headlines and decks, and use regular em dashes (—, made by hitting ctrl/shift/+) in precedes and sideheads. Don't use nicknames or first names of persons just to save space in a headline. When headlines are reprinted, small caps, without quotation marks, may be used for effect, but in letters to the editor, write article titles in caps and lowercase, with quotation marks.

UP-STYLE HEADLINES. In headlines and subheads that use "up" style, capitalize all words except the articles *a, an,* and *the;* the conjunctions *and, but, or, as,* and *if;* prepositions of three letters or fewer; and the second element of "permanent" compound words (those found in the dictionary): So-called Social Security, but Tough-Love Therapy. Capitalize adverbs that form an integral part of a verb: Japan Holds On to Islands, Taking Off for Australia, Jumping Up and Down, Potter Ran Up a Tab, but Duschene Ran up the Road (*up* is a preposition). Capitalize the first and last words of such headlines, including articles, conjunctions, and prepositions, no matter how short they are.

head-on (adjective and adverb). a head-on crash; the cars met head-on.

headquarters is plural, but it often takes a singular verb: The headquarters is in St. Louis.

head to head. They stood head to head, but a head-to-head battle.

heaven

heavenly bodies. Planets, stars, constellations, etc., are capitalized; the generic portions of the names are generally lowercase: the constellation Cassiopeia, Arcturus, Satellite VII of Jupiter, Mars's moon Phobos (Phobos, one of Mars's moons), Hale-Bopp comet, the Crab nebula, the Magellanic clouds.

hectare. Abbreviation, ha, is acceptable after first reference and in charts and tables.

hedging. When dealing with breaking news, pay particular attention to tenses and qualifying phrases so that the article will not sound silly because of something that happens between when the magazine goes to press and when it reaches readers. See THIS WEEK.

height. Use figures. She was 5 feet, 2 inches tall; a 5-foot, 2-inch woman; she is 5 foot 2; a 5-foot-2 guard. Acceptable when the meaning is clear: Las Vegas's point guard stood 5-2.

hell, but Hades

hemisphere, the Western Hemisphere (the hemisphere)

her, hers, she. Do not use for countries, ships, or hurricanes. Use *it, its.*

herculean. Lowercase except when referring to Hercules.

hertz (Hz). See METRIC SYSTEM.

he or she. With ingenuity, most sentences can be gracefully and accurately reworded to avoid such constructions as "he or she," "him or her," and "his or hers." When an indefinite antecedent could be male or female, try the possible solutions below, as a last resort using *he or she* or, when that is cumbersome, *he* by itself. Helpful suggestions for avoiding *he or she* constructions can be found in *The Handbook of Nonsexist Writing* by Casey Miller and Kate Swift (Harper & Row, 1983), *The Nonsexist Word Finder* by Rosalie Maggio (Oryx Press, 1987), and *Guidelines for Bias-Free Writing* by Marilyn Schwartz et al. (Indiana University Press, 1995). Alternatives to using the generic *he* include:

- Dropping the pronoun.
- Repeating the noun.
- Replacing the noun with a synonym.
- Shifting to first person, second person, or "one."
- Using plurals.

CHANGE:

An employee who abuses his sick leave risks alienating his boss.
TO:
An employee who abuses sick leave risks alienating the boss.
OR:
Employees who abuse sick leave risk alienating their boss.

When a child stubs his toe, it's painful for everyone involved.
TO:
When a child stubs a toe, it's painful for everyone involved.

A person can't always tell when his best friend is telling the truth.
TO:
You can't always tell when your best friend is telling the truth.
OR:
One can't always tell when a best friend is telling the truth.

If a driver gets enough tickets, he or she could lose his or her license.
TO:
Drivers who get enough tickets could lose their licenses.

The principal ordered each student to report to the nurse's office before he or she went home sick.

TO:

The principal ordered students to report to the nurse's office before they went home sick.

See FAIRNESS and GENDER BIAS.

H-hour

hideout (noun)

high court. Acceptable on second reference to Supreme Court. See SUPREME COURT.

highflier, highflying

high mass is sung, not held. See MASS.

high rate of speed is redundant. Write *high speed* unless you mean acceleration, which is the rate of increase in speed.

high school (noun and adjective)

high tech (noun), high-tech (adjective)

highway names. For interstate highways: Interstate 15, the interstate. On second reference, I-15 is acceptable. For other federal highways: U.S. 87. For state and local highways: Route 611, the route. For roads that use the designation *Highway:* Highway 1A, the highway. Capitalize a compass point when it is part of a roadway's name; lowercase when it merely indicates direction: Interstate 95 North, take Route 66 west.

Hill. Capitalize when it refers to Capitol Hill, but avoid overuse, which sounds jargonistic.

Hispanic is acceptable as a noun and as an adjective referring to people tracing their descent to Latin America, Spain, or Portugal: a Hispanic. Hispanics may be of any race, so don't write, for example, *Hispanics and whites.* Use instead *Hispanics and non-Hispanics* or, if further distinction is needed, for example, *Hispanics and non-Hispanic whites.* See CHICANO, ETHNIC IDENTIFICATION, and LATINO(S).

historic. Use a historic.

historic events. Many easily recognized events are capitalized: Boston Tea Party, Battle of Bull Run, the Long March. Follow the dictionary and individual entries in this book and in the electronic NAMES file. If there is a possibility the term will not be understood, it probably should be lowercased and explained.

historic/historical. Historic means history making; historical means pertaining to history: Columbus's historic voyage; the family took a historical ride through Genoa.

historic periods. Capitalize recognized terms: Elizabethan Age, Jazz Age, Mauve Decade, Renaissance, Age of Reason, Roaring Twenties, Restoration, Christian Era, but lowercase century: 20th century. See AGES AND ERAS.

HIV (human immunodeficiency virus). *HIV virus* is redundant.

HMO(s). Acceptable for health maintenance organization(s) when clear.

hoard/horde. As a noun, a hoard is a stash; as a verb, it means to store away. A horde is a wandering group or a swarm.

hold down (verb), hold-down (noun and adjective)

holidays. Capitalize holidays, special days, special weeks, etc.: Christmas, Easter Sunday, New Year's Eve, Christmas Eve, Christmas Day, Hanukkah, Good Friday, Holy Week, Passover, Ramadan, Lent, Independence Day, Fourth of July, Yom Kippur, Armistice Day, Mother's Day, Bastille Day, Veterans Day, Presidents Day, Election Day, Inauguration Day, National Safety Week, Earth Week.

Holland was the name of a country in the Holy Roman Empire and appears now in the names of two provinces in the Netherlands, which is the preferred name for that nation. Except in casual references, avoid using *Holland* to mean the entire country.

Holy Communion. See SACRAMENTS.

holy grail. Lowercase except in references to the chalice of medieval legend.

holy orders

Holy Week

home builder, home building (noun), home-building (adjective)

home schooling (noun), home-schooling (adjective), home-school (verb), home-schooler (noun)

homesite

homosexual (noun and adjective). The term may be applied to both men and women. See GAY.

honorable, the. Abbreviate, the Hon., before a full name. Use only in quoted matter.

honorific titles. Use the honorifics *Miss, Mr., Mrs.,* and *Ms.* only in quoted matter or when needed for clarity, as when husbands and wives need to be distinguished from each other: The Chubbs disagreed about little, although Mrs. Chubb favored decriminalization while Mr. Chubb supported prohibition. (Alternatively, the tone of a story may allow you to make such a distinction using the couple's first names.)

hopefully means "in a hopeful mood": He hopefully described the team's prospects. Do not use it to mean "It is to be hoped." Incorrect: *She said that, hopefully, the team would win.*

horde/hoard. See HOARD/HORDE.

horsepower. Abbreviation, hp, is acceptable after first reference.

horse racing

hotline, hot line. Use one word for direct lines of emergency communication and for telephone lines to social services. For literal meanings, use two words: Bush called the Kazakh president on the hotline. The Lyme disease hotline was soon overwhelmed. Use insulated gloves when working on a hot line.

hour(s). Abbreviate, hr., only in charts, maps, and tables. See TIME.

hourly-wage increase

House. Capitalize in reference to the U.S. House of Representatives and to a specific state's House of Delegates; lowercase as in houses of Congress, either house of Congress.

House of Commons, the Commons, the House

humvee. Lowercase the nickname for high-mobility multipurpose wheeled vehicle (HMMWV), which is the modern equivalent of the jeep. Capitalize the name of the commercial version, the Hummer.

hurricanes. Capitalize when personified: Hurricane Hugo (the hurricane). Use it, not *he* or *she*.

husband, wife. Use commas: Melissa brought her husband, Bob, home (unless she has more than one husband).

hyphen. There is wide disagreement over the many rules for hyphenation, and the exceptions often outnumber the rules. The guidelines below and those in the entry on compound words are aimed at promoting clarity without filling copy with unnecessary punctuation.

NATIONALITY COMBINATIONS: Italian-American, Italian-Americans, Japanese-American, African-American, Afro-American, **but** Latin American, Hispanic American, French Canadian.

NUMBERS from twenty-one to ninety-nine, when spelled out (as at the beginning of a sentence), are hyphenated.

FRACTIONS. Hyphenate a fraction when it is used as an adjective: two-thirds majority. Write as two words when it is used as a noun: two thirds of his fortune.

X-TO-Y COMBINATIONS: 15-to-20-year-olds. If these become too complicated, express them some other way: persons 15 to 20 years old.

COMPLEX VERBS. Follow the dictionaries on noun combinations used as verbs. Hyphenate made-up combinations:
You should horsewhip that fellow. (**dictionary**)
He blue-penciled my story mercilessly. (**dictionary**)
Woods three-putted the 17th hole. (**made-up**)

SUSPENDED HYPHENS. Put a space after the hyphen in such constructions as They climbed the third- and fourth-highest peaks **and** She produced the video- and audiotapes.

HOMOGRAPHS. Be alert to line breaks of words that have different pronunciations and meanings depending on how they are hyphenated: *record* (verb), *rec-ord* (noun); *pro-ject* (verb), *proj-ect* (noun); *pro-gress* (verb), *prog-ress* (noun). Incorrect hyphenation can be fixed with the discretionary-hyphen mark (ctrl -).

PREFIXES AND SUFFIXES are generally solid. Follow the dictionaries for words not in this book. For made-up words, hyphenate when a vowel would otherwise be doubled or a consonant tripled (pre-empire, anti-inflation, bell-like, but cooperate and coordinate); when sound or sense might be confused (pro-union); when a prefix is attached to a capitalized word (pre-Columbian, trans-Atlantic), and when a newly formed word resembles one with an established but different meaning (work included re-creation of the old tavern; she re-covered the chair with burlap).

H

SYLLABIFICATION. Follow the dictionary on line-end word breaks. (*Webster's New World Fourth Edition* shows only preferred breaks; for all acceptable breaks, consult the *Third Edition.*) See COMPOUND WORDS, DASH, FRACTIONS, and entries for particular words.

I. See WE.

ice age. Capitalize references to the Pleistocene Epoch; lowercase otherwise: Ice Age humans, but the latest ice age.

iced tea

ID. Acceptable for *identification* when the meaning is clear.

Idaho (ID in addresses. Otherwise abbreviate, Ida., only in a tight spot on charts, maps, or tables.)

Idahoan

identification. Do not identify people by race, religion, national origin, ethnicity, etc., unless the information is clearly pertinent to the story.

ill(-). As an adjective, it is usually hyphenated, even in the predicate: Kristen made an ill-advised move. It was ill-advised.

Illinois (Ill., IL in addresses)

Illinoisan

immigrate. People immigrate *to* and emigrate *from:* Troia immigrated to India; Arabet emigrated from Turkey.

impact. Don't use as a verb except in quotes.

imply/infer. Imply is to indicate; infer is to draw a conclusion.

Impressionism. Capitalize references to the styles of art and music exemplified by, for example, Monet and Debussy; lowercase general references. See CULTURAL DESIGNATIONS.

Inauguration Day, but inaugural address

in box

Inc. Do not set off with commas. It is not always needed. See COMPANY NAMES.

inch(es). Abbreviate, in., only in charts, maps, and tables.

incidents/incidence. *Incidents* are occurrences; *incidence* is a range or degree of occurrence (Lori counted seven incidents of fraud; The incidence of disease had increased).

income-tax payer, but taxpayer

income tax return

independent counsel. Capitalize when used as an official title before a name. Lowercase otherwise. Independent Counsel Erika Raitt. Titles of comparable state officials vary.

indexing. Use the letter-by-letter method, ignoring word spaces, hyphens, dashes, virgules, and apostrophes. Alphabetize *St.* and *Ste.* as they appear:

Dyke College	index numbers	Stanford
D'Youville	index, price	St. Anselm
hardback	New England	Trinity
hard bop	new-fashioned	Tri-State
hard-bound	St. Andrews	Venus

india ink

Indiana (Ind., IN in addresses)

Indianan

individual retirement account(s). IRA(s) is acceptable on first reference when clear.

Indochina, Indochinese

industrial revolution

infantry. Capitalize in a name; lowercase otherwise: 1st Infantry Division (1st Infantry), the infantry, an infantry officer.

infectious organisms are usually referred to by genus (capitalized) and species (lowercase), both italicized: *Staphylococcus aureus.* On second reference, the genus may be abbreviated: *S. aureus.* Some of these organisms have common names, which are roman. *Trichinella spiralis,* for example, may be referred to as trichinae, and *Escherichia coli* may be referred to as E. coli. Some bacteriologists use descriptive terms like meningococcus, pneumococcus, and typhoid bacillus, which are not part of the classification system and are roman, lowercase.

infinitives. Don't hesitate to split one when doing so makes for easier reading or better understanding.

inflammable means the same as flammable, so use the shorter word.

infra( ). Combines solid except before a capitalization or an *a*.

INF Treaty. Acceptable on second reference to Intermediate-range Nuclear Forces Treaty.

initials. When abbreviating parts of a name with letters, use a period: T. Paul Urbach, J. R. Ewing, F. A. O. Schwarz, putting a thin space between letters. But do not use periods after letters that are mere designations not standing for actual names: A said to B; the X group accused the Y organization. When using three initials in place of a name, make them solid: FDR, JFK. When using initials as a story credit, use a thin space, an en dash, periods, italics, and no spaces between the initials: *–R.J.N.*

institute. Capitalize in a name; lowercase alone: Maryland Institute College of Art, the institute. See COLLEGES AND UNIVERSITIES.

insure. Use with regard to insurance. Use *ensure* when the meaning is "to make sure" or "make safe," and *assure* when the meaning is "to promise confidently."

inter( ). Combines solid except before a capitalization.

International Court of Justice, World Court (the court)

Internet. On second reference, the Net is acceptable when the meaning is clear.

Interstate. Interstate 83, the interstate. I-83 is acceptable on second reference. See HIGHWAY NAMES.

intifada. Palestinian uprising in Gaza and the West Bank.

intra( ). Combines solid except before a capitalization, before an *a,* or in a confusing combination.

IOU(s)

Iowa (IA in addresses. Otherwise abbreviate, Ia., only in a tight spot on charts, maps, or tables.)

Iowan

IQ(s)

Iron Curtain

Islam. The Muslim religion. Members are Muslims, their deity is Allah, Mohammed is the prophet and "messenger," the mosque is the house of worship, and the holy day is Friday. Capitalize Prophet when it refers to Mohammed. Note: Although Arabic is the language of the Koran, the Islamic holy book, not all Arabs are Muslims and not all Muslims are Arabs. For instance, most Turks and Iranians are Muslims, but they are not Arabs. The two major groups in Islam are Sunni and Shiite. Leadership titles include imam, mullah, hojatoleslam, ayatollah, sheik, and grand mufti. Organizations in the United States include the American Muslim Mission, which publishes the weekly *Muslim Journal* and whose leaders are addressed as imam, and the Nation of Islam, formerly the World Community of Islam in the West, which publishes the weekly *Final Call* and whose leaders are addressed as minister. See MUSLIM.

island(s). Capitalize when part of a name; lowercase otherwise: Mariana Islands (the islands).

isotopes. Use a hyphen: strontium-90, uranium-235.

italics. TITLES. Italicize the names of books, periodicals, newsletters, plays, movies, operas, oratorios, and other long musical compositions with distinctive names, radio and television series, ballets, paintings, sculpture, photographs, comic books, comic strips, collections of poetry, and long poems published separately.

PERIODICALS. Italicize the names of newspapers, magazines, and similar periodicals: *Daily Citizen, U.S.News & World Report (U.S. News, USN&WR)*. Italicize and capitalize *the* only when the name is used formally or officially, as in photo credits and tables, and *the* is part of the periodical's name: THE CAPITAL TIMES (as a photo credit), the *Capital Times* or the *Times* (in body type). Italicize the name of the city only when it is part of the official name: *La Crosse Tribune,* the Baltimore *Sun.* Capitalize and italicize *magazine* only if the word is part of the title: *New Orleans Magazine, Time* magazine.

FOREIGN WORDS. Italicize those designated as such by *Webster's New World College Dictionary* as well as words not in the dictionary but known to you as foreign. Do not italicize foreign proper nouns.

A WORD REFERRED TO AS A WORD ONLY, not used for its meaning, is italicized: He inserted an *and* into the record.

LEGAL CITATIONS are italicized: *Haley v. Oklahoma.*

PUNCTUATION marks generally take the font of the preceding word or character: "Louis directed it *[Whose Life Is It Anyway?]* in Baltimore." Exceptions are parentheses and brackets when the beginning or the end of the enclosed material is roman: "Louis directed it [the theatrical version of *Whose Life Is It Anyway?*] in Baltimore"; and question marks and exclamation marks when the marks are not part of an italicized title: Did Brooks direct *Broadcast News*?

POSSESSIVES. Set the apostrophe and the *s* roman: *U.S. News*'s *ethics guidelines.* See BOOK TITLES, MAGAZINES, MUSICAL COMPOSITIONS, NEWSPAPERS, SMALL CAPS, and TITLES OF WORKS.

its/it's. Its is the possessive of it; it's is the contraction for it is: It's easy to find your car when you spot its antenna. Avoid using it's for it has.

jargon

jail. Do not use interchangeably with prison. In general, jails house people who are awaiting trial or sentencing, who have been convicted of misdemeanors (with a sentence of less than a year), or who are confined for civil violations; prisons house convicted felons.

January. See DATES and MONTHS.

jargon. See SLANG, DIALECT, AND JARGON.

jeep. Lowercase generic descriptions of small military vehicles; capitalize when used as a trademark for DaimlerChrysler vehicles.

Jehovah. See DEITY.

Jewish congregations for the most part belong to one of four groups:
1. Union of American Hebrew Congregations (Reform)
2. United Synagogue of Conservative Judaism (Conservative)
3. Union of Orthodox Jewish Congregations of America (Orthodox)
4. Federation of Reconstructionist Congregations and Havurot (Reconstructionist)

Jewish houses of worship are temples or synagogues. Reform congregations generally use temple: Temple Beth El (the temple), but check the individual name. Conservative and Reconstructionist congregations generally use synagogue: Beth Israel Synagogue (the synagogue), but check the individual name. Orthodox congregations always use synagogue: Agudas Achim Synagogue (the synagogue). Titles are rabbi and cantor: Rabbi Samuel Silver (Rabbi Silver, Silver, the rabbi); Cantor Ralph Orloff (Cantor Orloff, Orloff, the cantor). Rabbinical groups are the Central Conference of American Rabbis (Reform), the Rabbinical Assembly (Conservative), the Rabbinical Council of America (Orthodox), the Union of Orthodox Rabbis, and the Reconstructionist Rabbinical Association.

jibe/gibe. Jibe is to be in agreement or to shift sails; gibe is to jeer or taunt.

Joint Chiefs of Staff, Joint Chiefs, the chiefs of staff, the chiefs

Jr. Do not set off with commas: Anthony Soprano Jr. went to the ocean. Generally, it is not necessary to use *Jr.* unless there is the danger of confusion between a living father and son or unless a person is well known by the *Jr.*

judge. Capitalize before a name; lowercase otherwise: Appeals Court Judge Helen Nies (appellate Judge Nies, federal Judge Nies, Judge Nies, the judge).

judgment/verdict/settlement. A verdict is rendered by a judge or a jury, and it can result in a judgment, which is "awarded" by a civil court. A settlement, which is "reached" or "agreed to," is a voluntary agreement by both sides in a civil trial.

July. Do not abbreviate except in charts and tables. See DATES and MONTHS.

June. Do not abbreviate except in charts and tables. See DATES and MONTHS.

juris doctor (J.D.) is the basic law school degree, which formerly was usually the bachelor of laws degree (LL.B.). Other law degrees include master of laws (LL.M.), master of comparative law (M.C.L.), and doctor of juridical science (S.J.D.). The doctor of laws degree (LL.D.) is often an honorary degree.

just( ). Do not hyphenate in such constructions as a just completed project, a just published study.

justice. Capitalize before a name; lowercase otherwise: Associate Justice Sandra Day O'Connor (Justice Sandra Day O'Connor, Justice O'Connor, the associate justice, the justice).

king

Kansan

Kansas (Kan., KS in addresses)

kbps (1,000 bits per second). This measure of modem speed is acceptable on all references when the meaning is clear (56 kbps, a 56-kbps modem).

K.C. Generally limit its use as a nickname for Kansas City to quotes.

keep-away (noun)

( )keeper. Most combinations are solid, but some are two words. Follow the dictionaries: bookkeeper, gatekeeper, hotelkeeper, housekeeper, peacekeeper, record keeper, vigil keeper, zookeeper.

Kentuckian

Kentucky (Ky., KY in addresses)

Keogh plan(s)

keyword

kidnapping

kilo( ). Abbreviations for the following are acceptable after first reference and in charts and tables:

kilobit(s)—Kb
kilobyte(s)—K
kilogram(s)—kg
kilohertz—kHz
kiloliter(s)—kL
kilometer(s)—km
kilopascal(s)—kPa
kilowatt(s)—kW
kilowatt-hour(s)—kWh

king. Capitalize before a name; lowercase alone. Use roman numerals: King Bruno III (the king).

knock down (verb), knockdown (noun and adjective)

knot stands for nautical miles per hour, so don't write *knots per hour.*

Koran. See ISLAM.

Korean names are usually written as three words: Kim Dae Jung, with Kim the family name. Variations, most often used by Koreans living outside the Koreas, include Kim Dae-jung and Kim Daejung. Some Korean names are westernized, putting the family name last: Dae Jung Kim. Follow an individual's preference.

kudos is singular.

K

loath loathe

L.A. is acceptable on second reference to Los Angeles when the meaning is clear.

la, le, les. See FRENCH NAMES and PARTICLES.

Labrador. Abbreviate, Lab., only in charts, maps, and tables.

lady. Do not use as a synonym for woman.

lame duck (noun), lame-duck (adjective)

laserdisk

Latin American. Resident and adjective.

Latino(s) is acceptable as a noun and adjective for people of Spanish-speaking or Latin American descent. When deciding whether to apply *Latino, Hispanic, or Chicano* to particular individuals or groups, take personal preference into account. See CHICANO and HISPANIC.

law. Lowercase, even in a name: the immigration and nationality law, but the Corn Laws (because it's a historical term).

law degree. See JURIS DOCTOR.

law school. See COLLEGES AND UNIVERSITIES.

lectern/podium. A lectern is a stand that holds a speaker's notes; a podium is a platform that a speaker stands on.

left. Lowercase unless it is part of the official name of a political party: the left wing of the party, a left-wing caucus. Don't use *left-winger* except in quoted matter.

left-handed

legal advice. See FAIRNESS.

legal citations. Italicize: *Brunowski v. Minnesota.*

legislature. Capitalize when it is the name of the body; lowercase otherwise: Idaho Legislature (the Legislature), Massachusetts legislature (the actual name is the General Court), the Montana and Mississippi legislatures.

lesbian. See GAY and HOMOSEXUAL.

less measures volume, not numbers: less corn, fewer birds. When writing about ratios and percents, use *fewer* when dealing with things that can be counted (except when less than 1), *less* when dealing with quantity: fewer than 3 in 10 editors attend seminars; less than 1 nurse in 6 lives nearby; fewer than 50 percent of the company's employees are graduates; less than 50 percent of the company's workforce is covered.

liberal. Capitalize when referring to a political party; lowercase when designating a person's political position. Since the term often reflects a writer's individual judgment and may not correspond to a reader's, it is best to reserve it for cases in which there is widespread agreement. Where feasible, be more specific: Senator Moltisanti usually voted with the proponents of abortion funding.

lieutenant governor. Capitalize and abbreviate before a full name; capitalize and spell out before a last name only; lowercase and spell out otherwise: Lt. Gov. Lyle Betts (Lieutenant Governor Betts, the lieutenant governor).

lift off (verb), liftoff (noun)

liftouts. See QUOTATIONS.

like, as. *Like* is a perfectly good substitute for *such as,* and it is more succinct: The table was full of goodies, like apples and candy. *Like* is also correct when it is used as a preposition: Her voice sounds like a machine gun. However, *as,* not *like,* must be used when it is a conjunction introducing a clause: I feel well, as I knew I would.

( )like. As a suffix, write it solid except when it is used with proper names (Lincoln-like), in the case of a doubled *l* (jail-like), with an abbreviation (ATM-like), or when using hyphenated combinations (theme-park-like).

likely (adjective). The Terps are likely to win. Do not use as an adverb unless it is preceded by *most, quite,* or *very:* He most likely will go.

links. Also called hotlinks or hyperlinks. On Web pages, use roman type; on paper pages, use italics.

CONSISTENCY. Make side links within a particular Web page either all sentences or all fragments.

PUNCTUATION. Put quotation marks, apostrophes, periods, commas, etc., outside the link unless the punctuation is part of the language used in the link rather than the text surrounding it.

( ) list. the A list, A-list people.

lists, enumerations. Treat alike all numbers of a group's elements:

First, the Celts. Second, the Saxons. Third, the Normans.

1. The United States did not sign the treaty.
2. Congress acted without responsibility.

These were the steps that led to peace: (1) establishment of the base at Subic Bay, (2) issuance of the U.S. ultimatum, (3) acceptance of the ultimatum.

liter(s). L is acceptable after first reference and in charts and tables.

( )lived. a long-lived play; the play was long lived.

loath/loathe. Loath means reluctant; loathe means to detest.

locations. Capitalize special names of places, real and fanciful: the Rockies, the Smokies, the Promised Land, Twin Cities, Camelot, Badlands, the Windy City. For terms that are disparaging, politically subjective, or of debatable accuracy, use quotation marks or consider not using the term at all: "Hermit Kingdom," "Evil Empire." See GEOGRAPHIC NAMES and GEOGRAPHIC TERMS.

logon (noun), log on (verb). Janice used her corporate logon to log on to the intranet.

( )long. For combinations not listed here or in the dictionaries as solid, use a hyphen: hourlong, daylong, nightlong, weeklong, monthlong, yearlong, but decade-long, century-long, mile-long.

long-term (adjective). long-term advantage, but She did well in the long term.

longtime (adjective). longtime companions, but They lived together a long time.

Louisiana (La., LA in addresses)

Louisianian

lower. See CENTRAL.

lower 48. The contiguous states below the Canadian border.

low mass is recited, said, or read, not sung or held. See MASS.

LSD (the hallucinogen lysergic acid diethylamide). The abbreviation is acceptable on first reference if the context makes the meaning clear.

Ltd. Do not set off with commas. It is not necessary to use *Ltd.* if Co., Corp., Railroad, or other language clearly indicates a company name is used. See COMPANY NAMES.

lunchtime

Lutherans. Most Lutherans in the United States are organized into two major groups: the Evangelical Lutheran Church in America and the Lutheran Church–Missouri Synod. They work together through the Committee on Lutheran Cooperation, but the committee has no governing power. The form for referring to Lutheran pastors of all groups: the Rev. Henry Stromberg, pastor of First Lutheran Church (Pastor Stromberg, Stromberg). The Evangelical Lutheran Church in America is divided geographically into synods, headed by bishops. The Lutheran Church–Missouri Synod is divided into districts, headed by district presidents.

( )ly in multiple modifiers. When the first word is an adjective, use a hyphen; when it is an adverb, do not hyphenate: settling the hourly-pay issue, reporting a stunningly decisive victory.

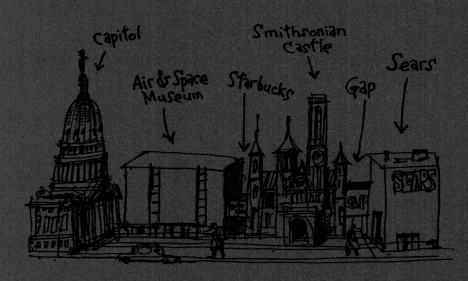

the Mall

( )made. Write solid if listed as such by the dictionary: handmade, home-made. Hyphenate made-up combinations used as adjectives: custom-made, factory-made, machine-made, but write as two words when used in the predicate: Her holster was machine made.

Mafia. Capitalize references to the secret criminal organization that originated in Sicily: The Gambino family controlled the Mafia's drug business. Lowercase references to similar organizations elsewhere: He was a lieutenant in the Russian mafia.

magazines. Italicize the names of magazines. Capitalize and italicize *magazine* only when it is part of the official name of the publication: *PC Magazine,* but *Time* magazine. Capitalize and italicize *the* only when the name is used formally, as in photo credits and tables, and is part of the magazine's name: THE NEW REPUBLIC (as a photo credit), but the *New Republic* (in body type). For readability, put all-cap names in caps and lowercase. See NEWSPAPERS and TITLES OF WORKS.

Magna Carta

Maine (ME in addresses. Otherwise abbreviate, Me., only in a tight spot on charts, maps, or tables.)

Mainer. A Maine resident or native.

major. Lowercase common nouns: journalism major, but English major. See COURSE TITLES.

majority. When used alone or with a prepositional phrase whose object is singular, it takes a singular verb: The majority backs the president. A majority of the class goes on to college. When the object of the prepositional phrase is plural, the verb may be singular or plural depending on the meaning: A majority of the students go on to college, but A majority of two students sends the measure to defeat.

majority leader. Capitalize as a title before a name; lowercase otherwise: Senate Majority Leader Carmela Farkas (Majority Leader Farkas; the Senate majority leader, Carmela Farkas).

major league (noun), major-league (adjective). Lowercase generic references to principal professional sports groups (he was a major-league linebacker), but capitalize trademarked references to baseball (the Major Leagues, Major League Baseball).

major-leaguers, little-leaguers

make over (verb), makeover (noun)

( )maker. Follow the dictionary on spelling. Make combinations not in the dictionary two words: automaker, boilermaker, bookmaker, carpet maker, decision maker, diemaker, dressmaker, filmmaker, image-maker, moviemaker, peacemaker, policymaker, speechmaker, steelmaker, toolmaker, troublemaker.

Mall, the. Capitalize the one in Washington, D.C.; for all others, lowercase *mall* when standing alone.

man. Seek and use alternatives to *man* when the meaning includes women.

TRADITIONAL EXPRESSION	POSSIBLE ALTERNATIVE
man the station	staff the station
man the barricades	mount the barricades
man should seek the truth	(people, we) should seek the truth
manpower	personnel, staff, workforce, human resources
manpowered flight	human-powered flight, muscle-powered flight
workmanlike	skillful
man-day, man-hour	work-day, work-hour

See GENDER BIAS.

manila envelope, hemp, paper, rope, etc.

Manitoba. Abbreviate, Man., only in charts, maps, and tables.

Manitoban

mantel/mantle. A mantel is the facing around a fireplace, including a shelf above; a mantle is a cloak or cape.

maps. See CAPTIONS, CHARTS AND TABLES, and PERCENT.

March. See DATES and MONTHS.

marine. Capitalize when referring to a particular country's organization: the U.S. Marine Corps (the Marine Corps, the U.S. Marines, the corps, a Marine regiment, a Marine sergeant, 15 Marine recruits finished training), the French Marine Corps, the U.S. and French marine corps. But

M

in references to members, if you could substitute the word *soldier, sailor,* or *airman* for *marine,* make it lowercase: 15 marines began training. **See** MILITARY TITLES.

Maryland (Md., MD in addresses)

Marylander

Mason-Dixon Line

mass, high mass, low mass. Masses are not "held." Mass is celebrated, read, or said. High mass is sung. Low mass is recited, said, or read.

Massachusetts (Mass., MA in addresses)

Massachusetts resident, native, etc. Also acceptable are Massachusettsan and Bay Stater.

master of arts (M.A.), master of arts degree, master's degree, a master's

May. See DATES and MONTHS.

mayor. Capitalize as a title before a name; lowercase otherwise: Mayor Leonard Andrews (Mayor Andrews, the mayor), a mayor.

M.D. (M.D.'s). See DOCTOR.

MDT. See TIME ZONES.

mean. See AVERAGE/MEAN/MEDIAN.

meat-ax (noun and adjective), meatcutter, meat grinder, meat wagon

medal. Capitalize with a specific name; lowercase for awards representing levels of victory in track meets, fairs, etc.: the Medal of Honor, the Good Conduct Medal, the silver medal in the pole vault.

Medal of Honor. Capitalize. (*Congressional* is not part of the name.)

medevac helicopter

media. Medium is singular; media is plural: The television medium is cool. The newspaper and magazine media are hot.

median. See AVERAGE/MEAN/MEDIAN.

Medicaid

medical terms. Diseases, conditions, and symptoms are roman and lowercase except for proper names they may contain: aneurysm, atherosclerosis, emphysema, Hodgkin's disease, hyperglycemia, infarction, measles, Ménière's syndrome, neuralgia, osteoarthritis, Parkinson's disease.

TESTS AND TREATMENTS also are generally lowercase and roman except for words that would be capitalized when alone: tuberculin test, barium X-ray, cobalt therapy, acupuncture, Heimlich maneuver, Pap smear, metabolism test.

IN NONMEDICAL CONTEXTS, take care not to misuse terms (schizophrenia, for instance, is not the same as split personality), and be vigilant when using terms describing medical conditions in a nonmedical context—which can be unnecessarily painful to people with such conditions and to those close to them. See DISABLED, HANDICAP, INFECTIOUS ORGANISMS, and VICTIM.

medigap. Nickname for Medicare supplement insurance, which is designed to pay most medical expenses not covered by Medicare.

mega( ). Combines solid except before a vowel: megabuck, megabyte, megadeath, megadose, mega-answer, mega-emergency.

megabyte. 1 megabyte, 16 megabytes, 16-megabyte disk. MB and megs are acceptable on second reference when the meaning is clear: 1MB, 16MB, 16MB disk, 16 megs.

member of Congress. See CONGRESSPERSON and PARTY DESIGNATION.

member of Parliament (M.P.). Capitalize before a name; lowercase otherwise: Member of Parliament Pip Smith, the member of Parliament. M.P. Pip Smith is acceptable if the context makes the title clear.

merchant marine. U.S. merchant marine, the merchant marine, but U.S. Merchant Marine Academy.

meter(s). Abbreviation, m, is acceptable after first reference and in charts and tables.

Methodists. See UNITED METHODIST CHURCH.

metric system. In general, use metric units when they are relevant in a story and would not confuse readers, as in technical references in articles about science and medicine. In nontechnical uses, however, readers are usually better served by traditional units, so when, for instance, a correspondent in Pretoria writes about hauling a 25-kilogram package along a 5-kilometer road, it is generally better to convert the weight to pounds and the distance to miles. In most cases, metric terms should be spelled out the first time they are used. Thereafter, abbreviation is acceptable. Metric abbreviations are not followed by a period. Some measures, such as those of guns, are abbreviated on first reference: 77-mm gun, 7.3-mm pistol, 35-mm film.

NAME	SYMBOL	APPROXIMATE SIZE OR EQUIVALENT
LENGTH		
meter	m	$39^1/_2$ inches
kilometer	km	.6 mile
centimeter	cm	.4 inch (width of a paper clip)
millimeter	mm	thickness of a paper clip
AREA		
hectare	ha	$2^1/_2$ acres
WEIGHT		
gram	g	weight of a paper clip
kilogram	kg	2.2 pounds
metric ton	t	long ton (2,240 pounds)
VOLUME		
liter	L	1 quart and 2 ounces
milliliter	mL	$^1/_5$ teaspoon
PRESSURE		
kilopascal	kPa	atmospheric pressure is about 100 kPa
TEMPERATURE		
Celsius	°C	$^5/_9$ °F after subtracting 32 from °F
freezing water	°C	32°F
boiling water	100°C	212°F
body temp.	37°C	98.6°F
ELECTRICITY		
kilowatt	kW	
kilowatt-hour	kWh	
megawatt	MW	
MISCELLANEOUS		
modem speed	kbps	1,000 bits per second
hertz	Hz	one cycle per second
millisecond	ms	

CAPITALS. Names of all units start with a lowercase letter except at the beginning of a sentence. Exception: In *degrees Celsius, degrees* is lowercase but *Celsius* is capitalized. Symbols for units are lowercase except for liter and units derived from the name of a person (*m* for *meter* but *W* for *watt, Pa* for *pascal, Hz* for *hertz,* etc.). Symbols for prefixes that mean a million or more are capped, and those for less than a million are lowercase (*M* for *mega, k* for *kilo,* but *K* for *kilobyte*).

PLURALS. Names of units are made plural only when the number that precedes them is more than 1. For example, *0.25 liter* or ¹/₄ *liter,* but *250 milliliters.* Symbols for units are never pluralized (*250 mL*).

SPACING. Generally, leave a space between the number and the symbol to which it refers (7 m; 31.4 kg, but 32°F, 260K, and 12MB).

PERIOD. Do not use a period with metric-unit names and symbols except at the end of a sentence.

CONVERSIONS. Follow reason: Don't include figures that imply more precision than is justified by the original data. For example, convert 36 inches to 91 centimeters and 40.1 inches to 101.9 centimeters, not 101.854.

DETAILS are in "NBS Guidelines for Use of the Metric System," a free booklet published by the National Institute of Standards and Technology.

M

COMMON PREFIXES

FACTOR	PREFIX	SYMBOL	NAME
1,000,000,000,000,000,000,000,000	yotta	Y	septillion
1,000,000,000,000,000,000,000	zetta	Z	sextillion
1,000,000,000,000,000,000	exa	E	quintillion
1,000,000,000,000,000	peta	P	quadrillion
1,000,000,000,000	tera	T	trillion
1,000,000,000	giga	G	billion
1,000,000	mega	M	million
1,000	kilo	k	thousand
100	hecto	h	hundred
10	deka	da	tenfold
1/10	deci	d	tenth
1/100	centi	c	hundredth
1/1,000	milli	m	thousandth
1/1,000,000	micro	u	millionth
1/1,000,000,000	nano	n	billionth
1/1,000,000,000,000	pico	p	trillionth
1/1,000,000,000,000,000	femto	f	quadrillionth
1/1,000,000,000,000,000,000	atto	a	quintillionth
1/1,000,000,000,000,000,000,000	zepto	z	sextillionth
1/1,000,000,000,000,000,000,000,000	yocto	y	septillionth

METRIC CONVERSION FACTORS (APPROXIMATE)

WHEN YOU KNOW	MULTIPLY BY	TO FIND	SYMBOL
LENGTH			
inches	2.54	centimeters	cm
feet	30	centimeters	cm
yards	.9	meters	m
miles	1.6	kilometers	km
AREA			
square inches	6.5	square centimeters	cm^2
square feet	.09	square meters	m^2
square yards	.8	square meters	m^2
square miles	2.6	square kilometers	km^2
acres	.4	hectares	ha
WEIGHT			
ounces	28	grams	g
pounds	.45	kilograms	kg
short tons (2,000 pounds)	.9	metric tons	t
VOLUME			
teaspoons	5	milliliters	mL
tablespoons	15	milliliters	mL
cubic inches	16	milliliters	mL
fluid ounces	30	milliliters	mL
cups	.24	liters	L
pints	.47	liters	L
quarts	.95	liters	L
gallons	3.8	liters	L
cubic feet	.03	cubic meters	m^3
cubic yards	.76	cubic meters	m^3
PRESSURE			
inches of mercury	3.4	kilopascals	kPa
pounds/square inch	6.9	kilopascals	kPa
TEMPERATURE (EXACT)			
degrees Fahrenheit	$5/9$ (after subtracting 32)	degrees Celsius	°C

(Explanations and tables in this section are taken from *Metric Style Guide for the News Media,* published by the National Institute of Standards and Technology, with adjustments for *USN&WR* style.) See TEMPERATURE and WEIGHTS AND MEASURES.

metric ton. 1,000 kilograms (about 2,200 pounds). Abbreviation, t, acceptable after first reference and in charts, maps, and tables.

Mexican-American. An American of Mexican origin. See CHICANO, HISPANIC, and LATINO.

Mexican names. See SPANISH-LANGUAGE NAMES.

Michigan (Mich., MI in addresses)

Michigander, but Michiganian traits or Michigan traits

mid( ). Usually written solid unless followed by a capitalization or a figure: midlife, midafternoon, midcentury, midocean, midrange, midseason, midsize, mid-Atlantic, mid-1980s, mid-'90s.

middle. See CENTRAL.

middle age (noun), middle-aged (adjective)

Middle Ages

Middle East. Authorities differ on the boundaries. For general use, it comprises Iran to Asiatic Turkey, including Egypt, Cyprus, and the Arabian Peninsula. Also sometimes included are Afghanistan, Sudan, Libya, Tunisia, Algeria, and Morocco. See NEAR EAST.

Mideast. Acceptable for Middle East.

Midwest. See POLITICAL REGIONS.

MI-5, MI-6. Britain's civilian intelligence agencies. MI-5 handles counterintelligence within Britain; MI-6 handles external espionage. Together they are the Special Intelligence Services.

MiG-25. See AIRCRAFT.

mike. Acceptable for microphone when the meaning is clear.

mil. Acceptable abbreviation for million(s) in charts, maps, and, tables.

mile. Abbreviation, mi., acceptable only in charts, maps, and tables.

miles per gallon (mpg). Abbreviation acceptable on all references.

miles per hour (mph). Abbreviation acceptable on all references.

military police (MP, MPs)

military titles. Abbreviate before a full name and, if necessary, in charts; spell out otherwise. Capitalize before a name; lowercase otherwise. A military title may be dropped on subsequent reference, but it is frequently useful to keep it. Abbreviations for service designations, USA (for U.S. Army), USNR (for U.S. Navy Reserve), etc., are acceptable with full name and rank: Lt. (j.g.) William Oliver, USNR.

COMMISSIONED OFFICERS

ARMY, MARINE CORPS, AIR FORCE

NAME OF RANK	BEFORE FULL NAME	BEFORE LAST NAME	IN LATER MENTION
General	Gen.	General	the general
Lieutenant General	Lt. Gen.	General	the general
Major General	Maj. Gen.	General	the general
Brigadier General	Brig. Gen.	General	the general
Colonel	Col.	Colonel	the colonel
Lieutenant Colonel	Lt. Col.	Colonel	the colonel
Major	Maj.	Major	the major
Captain	Capt.	Captain	the captain
First Lieutenant	1st Lt.	Lieutenant	the lieutenant
Second Lieutenant	2nd Lt.	Lieutenant	the lieutenant

NAVY, COAST GUARD

NAME OF RANK	BEFORE FULL NAME	BEFORE LAST NAME	IN LATER MENTION
Admiral	Adm.	Admiral	the admiral
Vice Admiral	Vice Adm.	Admiral	the admiral
Rear Admiral	Rear Adm.	Admiral	the admiral
Rear Admiral (Lower)	Rear Adm.	Admiral	the admiral
Captain	Capt.	Captain	the captain
Commander	Cmdr.	Commander	the commander
Lieutenant Commander	Lt. Cmdr.	Commander	the commander
Lieutenant (junior grade)	Lt. (j.g.)	Lieutenant	the lieutenant
Ensign	Ens.	Ensign	the ensign

Maj. Gen. Jesse Aument (General Aument, Aument, the general)

WARRANT OFFICERS

NAME OF RANK	BEFORE FULL NAME	BEFORE LAST NAME	IN LATER MENTION
Chief Warrant Officer 2, 3, and 4	Chief Warrant Officer	Chief Warrant Officer	the warrant officer
Warrant Officer	Warrant Officer	Warrant Officer	the warrant officer

Chief Warrant Officer Kenneth Brown (Chief Warrant Officer Brown, Brown, the warrant officer)

ENLISTED RANKS

ARMY

Sergeant major of the Army follows the name: Charles MacDowell, sergeant major of the Army (Sergeant MacDowell, MacDowell, the sergeant).

BEFORE FULL NAME	BEFORE LAST NAME ONLY
Command Sgt. Maj.	Sergeant
Sgt. Maj.	Sergeant
1st Sgt.	Sergeant
Master Sgt.	Sergeant
Sgt. 1st Class	Sergeant
Staff Sgt.	Sergeant
Sgt.	Sergeant
Cpl.	Corporal
Spc.	Specialist
Pfc.	Private
Pvt.	Private

Command Sgt. Maj. Perry Sassoon (Sergeant Sassoon, Sassoon, the sergeant)

MARINE CORPS

Names of ranks in the Marine Corps follow the Army model and should be treated in the same way, although the named ranks do not always correspond.

TWO EXCEPTIONS:

BEFORE FULL NAME	BEFORE LAST NAME ONLY
Master Gunnery Sgt.	Sergeant
Lance Cpl.	Corporal

NAVY, COAST GUARD

Master chief petty officer of the Navy follows the full name: John Paul Smith, master chief petty officer of the Navy (Chief Smith, Smith, the chief).

BEFORE FULL NAME	BEFORE LAST NAME ONLY
Master Chief Petty Officer	Chief
Senior Chief Petty Officer	Chief
Chief Petty Officer	Chief

BEFORE FULL NAME	BEFORE LAST NAME ONLY
Petty Officer 1st Class	Petty Officer
Petty Officer 2nd Class	Petty Officer
Petty Officer 3rd Class	Petty Officer
Seaman	Seaman
Seaman Apprentice	Seaman
Seaman Recruit	Recruit

SPECIALTIES: The Navy and the Coast Guard have more than 75 types of specialists who are customarily referred to by their specialties. They range from boatswain's mate to electronics-warfare technician, and each specialty runs the scale of ranks from recruit to master chief. The hundreds of official abbreviations are meaningless to all but a few readers, so the only useful abbreviation is omission of a few words. Lowest rating of electronics-warfare technician, for instance, is Electronics Warfare Technician Seaman Recruit Manny Langston, but for our purposes he is Seaman Recruit Manny Langston, an electronics-warfare technician (Seaman Recruit Langston, Langston, the seaman recruit). Taking radioman as an example, the ratings are:

BEFORE FULL NAME	BEFORE LAST NAME	IN LATER MENTION
Master Chief Radioman	Chief	the chief
Senior Chief Radioman	Chief	the chief
Chief Radioman	Chief	the chief
Radioman 1st Class	Radioman	the radioman
Radioman 2nd Class	Radioman	the radioman
Radioman 3rd Class	Radioman	the radioman
Radioman Seaman	Seaman	the seaman
Radioman Apprentice	Apprentice	the apprentice
Radioman Recruit	Recruit	the recruit

Master Chief Radioman Bill Budd (Chief Budd, Budd, the chief)

Note: Specialists beginning with 3rd class hold the parallel ratings of petty officers, chief petty officers, etc.; nevertheless, they usually are styled by their specialties.

AIR FORCE

Chief master sergeant of the Air Force follows the name: Seth Wright, chief master sergeant of the Air Force (Chief Wright, Wright).

BEFORE FULL NAME	BEFORE LAST NAME ONLY
Chief Master Sgt.	Chief
Senior Master Sgt.	Sergeant
Master Sgt.	Sergeant
Technical Sgt.	Sergeant
Staff Sgt.	Sergeant

BEFORE FULL NAME	BEFORE LAST NAME ONLY
Sgt.	Sergeant
Senior Airman	Airman
Airman 1st Class	Airman
Airman	Airman
Airman Basic	Airman

See RETIRED.

military units. Use figures and capitalize long and short names: 101st Airborne Division (Air Assault), 101st Airborne Division, 101st Airborne, 6th Fleet, but the division, the airborne, the fleet. Use roman numerals for Army corps: V Corps, the corps. Capitalize and put quotation marks around nicknames: the "Screaming Eagles."

millennium(s). See CENTURY.

milliliter(s). Abbreviation, mL, acceptable after first reference and in charts and tables.

millimeter(s). Abbreviation, mm, acceptable after first reference and in charts and tables and in such familiar uses as 75-mm gun, 7.3-mm pistol, 35-mm camera.

million. When using numbers in millions, billions, or trillions, substitute the word for the zeros. Portions of a million, billion, or trillion may be shown in decimals, but except where necessary to show fine distinctions, round to no more than one digit after the decimal point: 8 million, 18 million, 12.3 billion, 1.5 trillion. If it is vital to go beyond one digit, up to three may be used. If exact numbers must be carried still further to show the desired information, use figures: 8,737,542; 7,346,507,000. Do not hyphenate when amounts are used adjectivally: a 15 million-gallon oil spill. Abbreviation, mil., is acceptable in charts, maps, and tables.

mine owner, minesweeper, mine worker

mini( ). Write solid except before a capitalization, before an *i*, or in a difficult-to-read combination: minibus, ministate, mini-apology.

minister. Capitalize as in Finance Minister, etc., before a name; lowercase otherwise: Finance Minister Robert Feustal, the finance minister, finance ministers.

ministry. Capitalize in the name of a primary agency of government; lowercase alone: the Russian Foreign Ministry, the Foreign Ministry, the ministry.

Minnesota (Minn., MN in addresses)

Minnesotan

minority leader. Capitalize as a title before a name; lowercase otherwise.

minuscule

minus sign. Use an en dash.

minute(s). Abbreviate, min., only in charts, maps, and tables. Spell out nine and below; use figures for 10 and above. See NUMBERS.

MIRV(s). Abbreviation for multiple independently targeted (or targetable) re-entry vehicle(s). Use only with an explanation.

Miss. See HONORIFIC TITLES.

missiles. See ROCKETS.

Mississippi (Miss., MS in addresses)

Mississippian

Missouri (Mo., MO in addresses)

Missourian

MIT. Acceptable on second reference to Massachusetts Institute of Technology.

mixed metaphors. Avoid such combinations as: *They went where the hand of man has never set foot.*

model. Capitalize with number and/or letter: Model 01W (the model).

Mohammed. Use this spelling for the Islamic prophet and for anyone named for him, except when the person is known to prefer a different spelling.

M-1. A measure of the U.S. money supply. M-1A, M-2, etc.

money. Use figures for sums of money, except when they begin a sentence. They are usually treated as singular: $4, $450, $4 million, 7 cents, a $4.3 million loan. Fifty thousand dollars was appropriated. About $50 million was stolen. Change foreign currency to the equivalent in U.S. dollars where possible. See CURRENCIES.

( )monger. Make combinations one word except when the *m* is doubled: rumormonger, but room-monger.

monsignor. Msgr. Bruno Dowla (Monsignor Dowla, the monsignor).

Montana (Mont., MT in addresses)

Montanan

month. Abbreviate, mo., only in charts, maps, and tables.

months. Use these abbreviations when they appear with a date and year: Jan., Feb., Aug., Sept., Oct., Nov., Dec. Do not abbreviate the month when standing alone or when used with the year only or the day only. In general, do not abbreviate months with five letters or fewer. But abbreviations or initial letters, where clear in meaning, may be used in charts, maps, and tables. See DATES.

monuments. Capitalize names: Jefferson Memorial, Brandenburg Gate, Statue of Liberty, Washington Monument (the monument).

moon. See HEAVENLY BODIES.

more than. See OVER.

Mormons. The official name is the Church of Jesus Christ of Latter-day Saints. Members may be referred to as Mormons or Latter-day Saints. A branch is a small congregation, a ward is a large congregation, and a stake is a district made up of a number of congregations. The two divisions of the priesthood are the Aaronic and the Melchizedek. The offices of the Aaronic priesthood, beginning with the lowest, are deacon, teacher, priest, and bishop. The offices in the Melchizedek priesthood are elder, seventy, high priest, patriarch, and apostle. A person of any ranking from elder up may be referred to as elder. President Walter Beitz of the Riverdale Stake (Elder Beitz, Beitz). President John Smith of the

Homeville Branch (President Smith, Elder Smith, Smith, the president). Bishop John Smith of the Centerton Ward (Bishop Smith, Elder Smith, Smith, the bishop). At church headquarters, the presiding officer is the first president. The first president and two counselors form the First Presidency; under the First Presidency is the Council of Twelve Apostles, also called the Quorum of Twelve Apostles; under the Twelve is the First Quorum of the Seventy, followed by the Second Quorum of the Seventy. Any member of these groups may be referred to as elder: Elder John Smith, an apostle and member of the Quorum of Twelve (Elder Smith, Smith). An additional body is the Presiding Bishopric, composed of the presiding bishop and two counselors and reporting directly to the first president. The bishopric has responsibility for temporal affairs. Its members are addressed as Bishop: Bishop Allison Young (Bishop Young, the bishop, Young).

The Reorganized Church of Jesus Christ of Latter Day Saints (note *Day* is capitalized and *Latter Day* has no hyphen) changed its name, effective April 6, 2001, to the Community of Christ. Members worship in local congregations. Congregations are responsible to district presidents; district presidents report to regional administrators, and regional administrators to the Council of Twelve Apostles. Certain geographical areas operate within a Mission Center system, in which congregations report to Mission Center presidents, and Mission Center presidents report to the Council of Twelve Apostles. The Council of Twelve Apostles reports to the First Presidency, made up of the president/prophet and two counselors. An additional body is the Presiding Bishopric, composed of the presiding bishop and two counselors who also report directly to the First Presidency. The two divisions of priesthood are the Aaronic and the Melchizedic. The Aaronic priesthood offices include deacon, teacher, and priest. Melchizedic offices are elder, seventy, high priest, evangelist, bishop, and apostle.

Moslem. See MUSLIM.

most favored nation (noun), most-favored-nation (adjective)

Most Rev. the Most Rev. Jimmy Jones (Archbishop Jones, the archbishop, Jones).

Mother's Day

Mount. Do not abbreviate except in charts, maps, and tables.

mountain. Capitalize when part of a name; lowercase alone: Rocky Mountains (the mountains), Sand Mountain (the mountain). Note: *sierra* means mountains, so don't write, for instance, *Sierra Nevada Mountains.* Write Sierra Nevada, Sierra Nevada range, Sierras.

Mountain states. See POLITICAL REGIONS.

mouse. The plural is mice, for both the furry and plastic versions.

movements. Lowercase except when they are derived from proper names: democracy, communism, Marxism, Marxist, conservative thought, Conservative (Party) platform.

moviemaking

movie ratings. G, PG, PG-13, R, NC-17, movies rated R and PG-13, a PG-rated movie. See SMALL CAPS.

movies, titles of. Italicize. Capitalize principal words and prepositions and conjunctions of more than three letters. For readability, make all-cap and all-lowercase titles, except acronyms, caps and lowercase.

MP(s). Acceptable on first reference to military police or military police officer(s) when the meaning is clear.

M.P. Member of Parliament. See MEMBER OF PARLIAMENT.

mpg. Acceptable on all references to miles per gallon.

mph. Acceptable on all references to miles per hour.

Mr., Mrs., Ms., Miss. See HONORIFIC TITLES.

MREs. Acceptable on second reference to meals ready to eat.

MST. See TIME ZONES.

mujahideen. Islamic warriors.

multi( ). Write solid except before an *i* or a capitalization.

multimillion-dollar (adjective)

multiple modifiers. See COMPOUND WORDS and HYPHEN.

musical compositions. Capitalize the main words. Use italics for the non-technical parts of titles of long compositions: Mozart's Symphony No. 41 in C Major, Mozart's *Jupiter* Symphony, Schubert's Eighth Symphony, Copland's *Appalachian Spring,* Bartok's Piano Concerto No. 3. Use italics for names of albums: *Frankie Ford's Oldies but Goodies, Volume 3.* Make names of songs roman with quotes: "Here Comes the Sun." See TITLES OF WORKS.

Muslim. Use Muslim and Islam, not *Moslem* and *Mohammedan,* in references to the religion. Do not use the term *Black Muslim* except as a historical term or when quoting someone. See ISLAM.

mutual funds. The first source for a fund's name is the *Investor's Mutual Fund Guide,* from Investment Company Data. For a fund too new to be in the guide, which is updated monthly, use the particular fund's prospectus. The Investment Company Institute's annual *Guide to Mutual Funds* is a useful source for a fund's entire name.

FUND. Include *Fund* when it helps identify a specific fund: Janus Fund, not *Janus,* but Janus Twenty. Fidelity Fund, but Fidelity Magellan.

FAMILY NAME. Include it in charts and tables and, unless it is otherwise clear from context, in running copy: Fidelity Magellan, not *Magellan.*

CATEGORIES. In describing a fund's type or its investment objective, use the categories in the *Investor's Mutual Fund Guide.* However, to save space, charts may use slightly different categories.

ABBREVIATION. When fund names must be shortened, first drop nonessential words, then abbreviate, but never so much that identification of the fund becomes difficult: Fidelity Select Portfolios Biotechnology Portfolio could become Fidelity Select Biotechnology or, if space is especially tight, such as in charts or tables, Fidelity Sel. Biotech. (but not, for example, *Fid. Sl. Bio.*).

PUNCTUATION. Do not use colons, hyphens, or dashes unless confusion could result otherwise: Mutual Beacon, not *Mutual: Beacon;* Fidelity Select Health Care, not *Fidelity Select–Health Care,* but Oregon Tax-Exempt Series. Use periods with abbreviations.

STINKY, T-BONE, FATS, & THE TORTMASTER LLP

nicknames

NAACP. Abbreviation for the National Association for the Advancement of Colored People. May be used on first reference in a tight lead, but the name should be spelled out as soon as possible.

names of persons. Use whatever name a person is known by, whether the name was received at birth, adopted legally, or taken informally for professional purposes, such as a stage name, pen name, or nom de guerre. When a newsworthy person changes names, use both names until readers become familiar with the new name. Use the spellings in this book and the electronic NAMES list, then consult the following:

1. *Webster's New World College Dictionary* (Macmillan)
2. *Webster's New Biographical Dictionary* (Merriam-Webster)
3. *Who's Who in America* and *Who Was Who in America*
4. *Current Biography,* the *Britannica* and *Americana* encyclopedias, and the *Political Handbook of the World*

Consult the electronic NAMES list for specific personal and company names. For the sake of clarity, capitalize initial letters even if the individual does not: E. E. Cummings, K. D. Lang. Do not use a person's given name alone in headlines or on second reference in a story unless there is a compelling reason to do so, such as if the person is very young or to distinguish brothers and sisters or spouses from each other.

FOREIGN NAMES. Aid can be had from the country desks of the State Department, from the *United States Department of State Diplomatic List,* and from the CIA's *Chiefs of State and Cabinet Members of Foreign Governments.* In using these sources, however, apply *U.S. News* rules for the country in question. See ARABIC NAMES, BRAZILIAN NAMES, CHINESE NAMES, FRENCH NAMES, GERMAN NAMES, HONORIFIC TITLES, NICKNAMES, PARTICLES, PORTUGUESE NAMES, RUSSIAN NAMES, SPANISH-LANGUAGE NAMES, and the electronic NAMES list.

NASA. Acceptable in all references to the National Aeronautics and Space Administration when clear.

Nasdaq. (Formerly NASDAQ.) Acceptable on all references to the Nasdaq Stock Market Inc.

nation, national. Capitalize in a name; lowercase otherwise: National Urban Coalition, the national government.

national anthem, but "The Star-Spangled Banner"

National Assembly. Capitalize when it is the actual name of a body: French National Assembly (the National Assembly, the Assembly). See ASSEMBLY.

national chairman. Capitalize when used as a title before the name of a head of a political party; lowercase otherwise: Democratic National Chairman Anthony Medina, the Democratic national chairman.

national committee. Capitalize in the full name of a political party's organization; lowercase otherwise: the Republican National Committee (the GOP National Committee, the national committee, the committee).

national committeeman(woman). Capitalize as a title before a name; lowercase otherwise: National Committeewoman Marianne Sunshine (the national committeewoman).

national convention of a political party. Capitalize in the full name; lowercase otherwise: the Democratic National Convention (the Democratic convention, the national convention, the convention).

National Guard. Capitalize when referring to a particular state's or nation's organization: the Utah National Guard (the National Guard, the Guard, a national guardsman, a guardsman).

national monument, site, park, etc. Capitalize in a name; lowercase otherwise: Montezuma Castle National Monument, the national monument; Eleanor Roosevelt National Historic Site, the historic site; Saratoga National Historical Park, the historical park.

National Park Service, the park service, the service

National Safety Week

Nation of Islam. See ISLAM.

nations and regions. Spell out whenever possible. The following abbreviations may be used in tight situations, but only in charts, maps, and tables.

REGION	RESIDENT	ADJECTIVE	ABBREVIATION
Afghanistan	Afghan(s)	Afghan	Afgh.
Albania	Albanian(s)	Albanian	Alb.
Algeria	Algerian(s)	Algerian	Alg.
American Samoa	Samoan(s)	Samoan	Am. Sam.
Andorra	Andorran(s)	Andorran	And.

REGION	RESIDENT	ADJECTIVE	ABBREVIATION
Angola	Angolan(s)	Angolan	Ang.
Anguilla	Anguillan(s)	Anguillan	Angu.
Antigua and Barbuda	Antiguan(s) and Barbudan(s)	Antiguan and Barbudan	Ant., Barbu.
Argentina	Argentine(s)	Argentine	Arg.
Armenia	Armenian(s)	Armenian	Arm.
Aruba	Aruban(s)	Aruban	Aru.
Australia	Australian(s)	Australian	Austral.
Austria	Austrian(s)	Austrian	Aust.
Azerbaijan	Azerbaijani(s)	Azerbaijani	Azer.
Bahamas	Bahamian(s)	Bahamian	Bah.
Bahrain	Bahraini(s)	Bahraini	Bahr.
Bangladesh	Bangladeshi(s)	Bangladeshi	Bngl.
Barbados	Barbadian(s)	Barbadian	Barb.
Belarus	Belarussian(s)	Belarussian	Bela.
Belau	Belauan(s)	Belauan	Belau
Belgium	Belgian(s)	Belgian	Belg.
Belize	Belizean(s)	Belize	Belz.
Benin	Beninese	Beninese	Benin
Bermuda	Bermudan(s)	Bermudan	Berm.
Bhutan	Bhutanese	Bhutanese	Bhu.
Bolivia	Bolivian(s)	Bolivian	Bol.
Bosnia and Herzegovina	Bosnian(s)	Bosnian	Bos.
Botswana	Botswana (plural: Batswana)	Botswanan	Bots.
Brazil	Brazilian(s)	Brazilian	Braz.
Britain	Briton(s), British	British	Brit.
British Virgin Islands	Resident of Virgin Islands	British Virgin Island	B.V.I.
Brunei	Bruneian(s)	Brunei	Bru.
Bulgaria	Bulgarian(s)	Bulgarian	Bulg.
Burkina Faso	Burkinabe	Burkinabe	Burk.
Burma	Burmese	Burmese	Burm.
Burundi	Burundian(s)	Burundian	Burundi
Cambodia	Cambodian(s)	Cambodian	Camb.
Cameroon	Cameroonian(s)	Cameroonian	Camr.
Canada	Canadian(s)	Canadian	Can.
Cape Verde	Cape Verdian(s)	Cape Verdian	C.V.
Cayman Islands	Caymanian(s)	Caymanian	Cay. Is.
Central African Republic	Central African(s)	Central African	C.A.R.
Chad	Chadian(s)	Chadian	Chad
Chile	Chilean(s)	Chilean	Chile
China	Chinese	Chinese	China
Colombia	Colombian(s)	Colombian	Col.

REGION	RESIDENT	ADJECTIVE	ABBREVIATION
Comoros	Comorian(s)	Comorian	Com.
Congo, Democratic Republic of the	Congolese	Congolese	Dem. Congo
Congo, Republic of the	Congolese	Congolese	Congo
Costa Rica	Costa Rican(s)	Costa Rican	C.R.
Croatia	Croat(s), Croatian(s)	Croatian	Croat.
Cuba	Cuban(s)	Cuban	Cuba
Cyprus	Cypriot(s)	Cypriot	Cyprus
Czech Republic	Czech(s)	Czech	Czech
Denmark	Dane(s)	Danish	Den.
Djibouti	Djiboutian(s)	Djiboutian	Djib.
Dominica	Dominican(s)	Dominican	Dmica.
Dominican Republic	Dominican(s)	Dominican	Dom. Rep.
East Timor	East Timorese	East Timorese	E. Tim.
Ecuador	Ecuadoran(s)	Ecuadoran	Ecua.
Egypt	Egyptian(s)	Egyptian	Egypt
El Salvador	Salvadoran(s)	Salvadoran	El Salv.
Equatorial Guinea	Equatorial Guinean(s)	Equatorial Guinean	Eq. Guin.
Eritrea	Eritrean(s)	Eritrean	Erit.
Estonia	Estonian(s)	Estonian	Est.
Ethiopia	Ethiopian(s)	Ethiopian	Eth.
Falkland Islands	Falkland Islander(s)	Falkland Island	Falk. Is.
Faeroe Islands	Faeroese	Faeroese	Faer. Is.
Fiji	Fijian(s)	Fijian	Fiji
Finland	Finn(s)	Finnish	Fin.
France	the French, Frenchman(men, woman, women)	French	France
French Guiana	Guianan(s), Guianese	Guianan	Fr. Gui.
Gabon	Gabonese	Gabonese	Gabon
Gambia	Gambian(s)	Gambian	Gam.
Georgia	Georgian(s)	Georgian	Geor.
Germany	German(s)	German	Germ.
Ghana	Ghanaian(s)	Ghanaian	Ghana
Gibraltar	Gibraltarian(s)	Gibraltar	Gib.
Greece	Greek(s)	Greek	Gr.
Greenland	Greenlander(s)	Greenlandic	Green.
Grenada	Grenadian(s)	Grenadian	Grenada

N

REGION	RESIDENT	ADJECTIVE	ABBREVIATION
Guadeloupe	Guadeloupian(s)	Guadeloupe	Guad.
Guatemala	Guatemalan(s)	Guatemalan	Guat.
Guinea	Guinean(s)	Guinean	Guinea
Guinea-Bissau	Guinean(s)	Guinean	Guin.-Biss.
Guyana	Guyanese	Guyanese	Guy.
Haiti	Haitian(s)	Haitian	Haiti
Honduras	Honduran(s)	Honduran	Hond.
Hong Kong	Hong Kongese, Hong Kongian(s)	Hong Kong	H.K.
Hungary	Hungarian(s)	Hungarian	Hung.
Iceland	Icelander(s)	Icelandic	Ice.
India	Indian(s)	Indian	India
Indochina	Indochinese	Indochinese	Indochina
Indonesia	Indonesian(s)	Indonesian	Indon.
Iran	Iranian(s)	Iranian	Iran
Iraq	Iraqi(s)	Iraqi	Iraq
Ireland	Irishman(men, woman, women), the Irish	Irish	Ire.
Isle of Man	Manxman(men, woman, women), the Manx, Manx resident	Manx	Is. of Man
Israel	Israeli(s)	Israeli	Isr.
Italy	Italian(s)	Italian	It.
Ivory Coast	Ivoirian(s)	Ivoirian	Iv. Cst.
Jamaica	Jamaican(s)	Jamaican	Jam.
Japan	Japanese	Japanese	Jpn.
Jordan	Jordanian(s)	Jordanian	Jor.
Kashmir	Kashmiri(s)	Kashmirian	Kash.
Kazakhstan	Kazakh(s)	Kazakh	Kaz.
Kenya	Kenyan(s)	Kenyan	Ken.
Kirgizstan	Kirgiz	Kirgizian	Kirg.
Kiribati	Kiribatian(s)	Kiribatian	Kirib.
Kosovo	Kosovar(s)	Kosovar	Kos.
Kuwait	Kuwaiti(s)	Kuwaiti	Kuw.
Laos	Lao or Laotian(s)	Laotian or Lao	Laos
Latvia	Latvian(s)	Latvian	Lat.
Lebanon	Lebanese	Lebanese	Leb.
Lesotho	Mosotho (plural: Basotho)	Basotho	Lesotho
Liberia	Liberian(s)	Liberian	Liberia
Libya	Libyan(s)	Libyan	Lib.
Liechtenstein	Liechtensteiner(s)	Liechtenstein	Liech.
Lithuania	Lithuanian(s)	Lithuanian	Lith.
Luxembourg	Luxembourger(s)	Luxembourg	Lux.

REGION	RESIDENT	ADJECTIVE	ABBREVIATION
Macao	Macanese	Macaoan	Mac.
Macedonia	Macedonian(s)	Macedonian	Mace.
Madagascar	Malagasy	Malagasy or Madagascan	Madag.
Malawi	Malawian(s)	Malawian	Malawi
Malaysia	Malaysian(s)	Malaysian	Mal.
Maldives	Maldivian(s)	Maldivian	Mald.
Mali	Malian(s)	Malian	Mali
Malta	Maltese	Maltese	Malta
Marshall Islands	Marshallese	Marshallese	Mrsh. Is.
Mauritania	Mauritanian(s)	Mauritanian	Mauritania
Mauritius	Mauritian(s)	Mauritian	Mauritius
Mexico	Mexican(s)	Mexican	Mex.
Micronesia	Micronesian(s)	Micronesian	Micro.
Moldova	Moldovan(s)	Moldovan	Mold.
Monaco	Monacan(s)	Monacan	Mon.
Mongolia	Mongol(s)	Mongolian	Mong.
Montenegro	Montenegrin(s)	Montenegrin	Mont.
Morocco	Moroccan(s)	Moroccan	Mor.
Mozambique	Mozambican(s)	Mozambican	Moz.
Namibia	Namibian(s)	Namibian	Nam.
Nauru	Nauruan(s)	Nauruan	Nauru
Nepal	Nepalese	Nepalese	Nepal
Netherlands	Netherlander(s), Dutchman(men, woman, women), the Dutch	Netherlandish, Dutch, Netherlands	Neth.
New Zealand	New Zealander(s)	New Zealand	N.Z.
Nicaragua	Nicaraguan(s)	Nicaraguan	Nicar.
Niger	Nigerois	Niger	Niger
Nigeria	Nigerian(s)	Nigerian	Nigeria
North Korea	North Korean(s)	North Korean	N. Kor.
Norway	Norwegian(s)	Norwegian	Nor.
Oman	Omani(s)	Oman, Omani	Oman
Pakistan	Pakistani(s)	Pakistani	Pak.
Palestine	Palestinian(s)	Palestinian	Pal.
Panama	Panamanian(s)	Panamanian	Pan.
Papua New Guinea	Papua New Guinean(s)	Papua New Guinean	Pap. N. Gn.
Paraguay	Paraguayan(s)	Paraguayan	Para.
Peru	Peruvian(s)	Peruvian	Peru
Philippines	Filipino(s)	Philippine	Phil.
Poland	Pole(s)	Polish	Pol.
Portugal	Portuguese	Portuguese	Port.
Puerto Rico	Puerto Rican(s)	Puerto Rican	P.R.

N

REGION	RESIDENT	ADJECTIVE	ABBREVIATION
Qatar	Qatari(s)	Qatari	Qatar
Réunion	Réunionese	Réunionese	Réun.
Romania	Romanian(s)	Romanian	Rom.
Russia	Russian(s)	Russian	Russ.
Rwanda	Rwandan(s)	Rwandan	Rwanda
Samoa	Samoan(s)	Samoan	Samoa
San Marino	Sanmarinese	Sanmarinese	S. Mar.
São Tomé and Príncipe	São Toméan(s)	São Toméan	S. Tm. Prn.
Saudi Arabia	Saudi(s)	Saudi Arabian, Saudi	Saudi Ar.
Scotland	Scot(s), Scotsman (men, woman, women)	Scottish	Scot.
Senegal	Senegalese	Senegalese	Senegal
Serbia	Serb(s)	Serbian	Serb.
Serb Republic	Bosnian Serb(s)	Bosnian Serb	R.S.
Seychelles	Seychellois	Seychelles	Seych.
Sierra Leone	Sierra Leonean(s)	Sierra Leonean	S. Leone
Singapore	Singaporean(s)	Singaporean	Sing.
Slovakia	Slovak(s)	Slovak	Slvk.
Slovenia	Slovene(s)	Slovenian or Slovene	Slvn.
Solomon Islands	Solomon Islander(s)	Solomon Islander	Sol. Is.
Somalia	Somali(s)	Somali	Som.
South Africa	South African(s)	South African	S. Af.
South Korea	South Korean(s)	South Korean	S. Kor.
Spain	Spaniard(s)	Spanish	Sp.
Sri Lanka	Sri Lankan(s)	Sri Lankan	Sri Lan.
St. Kitts and Nevis	Kittitian(s), Nevisian(s)	Kittsian, Nevisian	St. Kt.-Nev.
St. Lucia	St. Lucian(s)	St. Lucian	St. Luc.
St. Vincent and the Grenadines	Vincentian(s)	Vincentian	St. Vin.-Gren.
Sudan	Sudanese	Sudanese	Sud.
Suriname	Surinamese	Surinamese	Sur.
Swaziland	Swazi(s)	Swaziland	Swaz.
Sweden	Swede(s)	Swedish	Sw.
Switzerland	Swiss	Swiss	Switz.
Syria	Syrian(s)	Syrian	Syr.
Taiwan	Taiwanese	Taiwanese	Taiwan
Tajikistan	Tajik(s)	Tajik	Taj.
Tanzania	Tanzanian(s)	Tanzanian	Tan.
Thailand	Thai(s)	Thai	Thai.
Togo	Togolese	Togolese	Togo

REGION	RESIDENT	ADJECTIVE	ABBREVIATION
Tonga	Tongan(s)	Tongan	Tonga
Trieste	Triestino(s)	Triestine	Triest.
Trinidad and Tobago	Trinidadian(s) for inhabitants generally; Tobagan(s)	Trinidadian, Tobagan	Trin. & Tob.
Tunisia	Tunisian(s)	Tunisian	Tun.
Turkey	Turk(s)	Turkish	Turk.
Turkmenistan	Turkman(men)	Turkmenian	Turkm.
Tuvalu	Tuvaluan(s)	Tuvaluan	Tuv.
Uganda	Ugandan(s)	Ugandan	Ug.
Ukraine	Ukrainian(s)	Ukrainian	Ukr.
United Arab Emirates Abu Dhabi Ajman Dubai Fujairah Ras al-Khaimah Sharjah Umm al-Qaiwain	Resident of United Arab Emirates or resident of individual state	United Arab Emirate	U.A.E.
Uruguay	Uruguayan(s)	Uruguayan	Uru.
U.S. Virgin Islands	Resident of the Virgin Islands	Virgin Island	V.I.
Uzbekistan	Uzbek(s)	Uzbek	Uz.
Vanuatu	Vanuatuan(s)	Vanuatuan	Van.
Vatican City State	Resident of Vatican City	Vatican	Vat.
Venezuela	Venezuelan(s)	Venezuelan	Venez.
Vietnam	Vietnamese	Vietnamese	Viet.
Wales	Welshman(men, woman, women), the Welsh	Welsh	Wales
Western Sahara	Western Saharan(s)	Western Saharan	W. Sahara
Yemen	Yemeni(s)	Yemeni	Yemen
Yugoslavia	Yugoslav(s)	Yugoslav	Yug.
Zambia	Zambian(s)	Zambian	Zam.
Zimbabwe	Zimbabwean(s)	Zimbabwean	Zim.

native American. A person born in the United States.

Native American. Use for references to American Indians only when it is the expressed preference of the organization or individual involved. Otherwise, use American Indian, Indian, or the name of the specific tribe.

NATO (North Atlantic Treaty Organization). The abbreviation is acceptable on all references when the meaning is clear.

NATO commands and titles. A typical command: Allied Forces Southern Europe. Supreme Allied Commander Europe is an official title, but it would generally be better to use, for example, Gen. Leo McGarry, supreme allied commander for Europe, or General McGarry, the NATO commander for Europe.

naval. Capitalize when part of a name; lowercase otherwise: Jacksonville Naval Air Station (the naval air station, the naval station), a naval officer.

Naval Reserve, the Reserve, Reserve duty, the Reserves, but reserves, reservists, when referring to individual members

Navy. Capitalize when referring to a particular country's organization: the U.S. Navy (the Navy, a Navy destroyer), the British Navy (the Navy), Navy Lt. Fred Arble, the U.S. and British navies, a navy.

NCO. Acceptable on second reference to noncommissioned officer.

near( ). a near antique, nearby, a near catastrophe, near miss, near beer, nearsighted, near silk, but a nearly perfect circle, a near-death experience.

Near East is a dated term and should be avoided. However, it may be used in historical or archaeological references to the countries near the eastern end of the Mediterranean Sea, including those in North Africa and the Balkans, specifically the area formerly controlled by the Ottoman Empire. See MIDDLE EAST.

Nebraska (Neb., NE in addresses)

Nebraskan

Negro(es). Some people use the word and some object. Do not use it for an individual unless you know it is acceptable. See BLACK and RACIAL DESIGNATIONS.

neo( ). Write combinations solid except before an *o* or a capitalization.

netherworld

Nevada (Nev., NV in addresses)

Nevadan

New Age. The definition is nebulous, so use the expression with care. Alternative terms that might apply better to the point being made include: holistic, nontraditional, alternative, unconventional, modern, radically different, the latest, faddish, meditative, soothing, ethereal, natural, philosophical, spiritual, and a new way of looking at old wisdom. See AGES AND ERAS.

New Brunswick. Abbreviate, N.B., only in charts, maps, and tables.

New Brunswicker

New Democrat. Capitalize when it is the official name of a party, but lowercase *new* and use quotation marks on first reference when it is not an official name: McLaughlin led Canada's New Democrats; Bayh mobilized the "new Democrats."

"new economy," "old economy." Write lowercase. Use quotation marks on first reference. Hyphenate when they are used as adjectives and are not in quotation marks.

New England states. See POLITICAL REGIONS.

newfound

Newfoundland. Abbreviate, Nfld., only in charts, maps, and tables.

Newfoundlander

New Hampshire (N.H., NH in addresses)

New Hampshirite

New Jersey (N.J., NJ in addresses)

New Jerseyite

New Mexican

New Mexico (N.M., NM in addresses)

New Orleanian

newsgroup. Online discussion group devoted to a particular topic.

newsletters, names of. Use italics, no quotes. See TITLES OF WORKS.

newspapers. Italicize names. Capitalize and italicize *the* only when it is part of the paper's name and when you use the entire name, as in photo credits and formal lists: THE NEW YORK TIMES (as a photo credit), but the *New York Times,* the *Times* (in body type). Italicize the name of the city, locality, or country only when it is part of the paper's name: the *Alamogordo Daily News,* but the Logan *Herald-Journal.* A reliable source for newspaper names is the *Editor & Publisher International Year Book.* See MAGAZINES and TITLES OF WORKS.

New World

new world order

New Year's Day, New Year's Eve

New York (N.Y., NY in addresses). When there is confusion as to whether the city or state is meant, write New York State or New York City.

New Yorker

nicknames. Use quotes the first time a nickname appears in a given article: Eric "Slowhand" Clapton. But when a person with a familiar nickname appears for the first time with the nickname only, quotes need not be used: Ma Rainey, Ted Kennedy. Do not quote nicknames on subsequent use unless there is danger of offense or confusion. Do not create nicknames simply to accommodate headline sizes, to affect a breezy style, or to belittle someone. Do not coin or use nicknames or appellations regarded as pejorative, such as *Moonie* or *pro-lifer.* See LOCATIONS.

no. Capitalize if it is in quotes; lowercase if not: She said "No." She said no.

No. Use for *number* in such expressions as the nation's No. 1 volleyball scorer; No. 2; Nos. 1 and 2; She was No. 1; He was the No. 2 draft pick.

Nobel. Nobel Peace Prize (the peace prize, a Nobel, the Nobel Prize in literature, a Nobel Prize, Nobel Peace Prizes, Nobel Prizes, Nobels).

nobility. Capitalize titles before names; lowercase otherwise: Queen Elizabeth, the queen; Rupert Moldeau, third earl of Avon, Moldeau. **Treat titles like** sir, dame, lord, lady, count, **and** countess **as you would honorifics, i.e., don't use them unless they are in direct quotations or are needed for clarity:** "Sir Paul McCartney" **(in a quotation);** Paul McCartney, McCartney; "Lady Elizabeth Waltz," Waltz. **See YOUR HONOR, TITLES OF PEOPLE.**

no-fly zone

non( ). Write solid except before a capitalization or in confusing combinations: nonstop, nonnuclear, non-Euclidean, non-oil, non-community-property states.

none. When referring to a quantity taken as a whole, use a singular verb: None of the water was drinkable. None of the 10 miles of road was passable. **When referring to numbered items, use a plural verb:** None of the bottles were full.

no-no. Plural: no-nos.

nor. See OR.

north, northern. See COMPASS DIRECTIONS.

North Carolina (N.C., NC in addresses)

North Carolinian

North Dakota (N.D., ND in addresses)

North Dakotan

Northwest Territories. Abbreviate, N.W.T., only in charts, maps, and tables.

nose to nose. They stood nose to nose; a nose-to-nose confrontation.

not only . . . but. Do not use a comma in such sentences as *She found that he was not only a musician but also a magician* unless the two parts form a compound sentence or unless confusion would otherwise result.

Nova Scotia. Abbreviate, N.S., only in charts, maps, and tables.

Nova Scotian

November. See DATES and MONTHS.

now. now married lawyer, the now legendary shortstop.

nuclear age

nuclear power plant

number. A number are; the number is. See NO.

numbered titles. Capitalize as in Article I (the article).

numbers. In general, spell out cardinal and ordinal numbers below 10. Use figures for numbers 10 and up unless they begin a sentence: nine salesmen; the eighth door; 10 hammers; the 10th year; 11th-hour reprieve; Twenty-eight years separated the events; The car has six cylinders, but a V-6 engine. Spell out a number after a colon if what follows the colon is a complete sentence: Result of his speech: Forty million voters switched. Switched by his speech: 40 million voters.

EXCEPTIONS. The following numbers should be in figures even when they are less than 10: scores; vote tabulations; ratios; percent and percentages; types of stocks and bonds; time of day and dates; weights; measures; ages of animate objects; military units; when a fraction is added to a number; when using millions, billions, etc.: They won by 5 runs; The score was 3-2; a 74-to-3 vote; a 5-to-1 ratio; 3 percent; 6 percentage points; seven 6s; 5 o'clock; June 4; 2 pounds; 5 feet; 8-year-old girl; 1st Army; $2^1/_2$ years; 4 billion fish.

ABUTTING NUMBERS that are normally written in figures may be spelled out if confusion might result otherwise: She filled 16 six-ounce glasses.

DIVIDING BETWEEN LINES. Do not divide a figure at the end of a line if there is any alternative, even rewriting. If a split is unavoidable, it should come after a comma: 350,437,-402.

MILITARY. Use figures for numerical designations of military units: 6th Fleet, 45th Division; use roman numerals for Army corps: VII Corps.

PLURALS OF NUMBERS. Form plurals by adding *s:* B-52s, 1940s, the '30s.

ROMAN NUMERALS. Use them to designate monarchs, popes, sequential personal names, ships, automobiles, wars, and treaties: King George III, Pope John Paul II, Josh Lyman II, the Laughing Lass III, Lincoln Mark IV, World War I, START II. When quoting a document that uses roman numerals, keep them roman:

I. Be there.
II. Be on time.
III. Stay late.

SERIES. Whenever numbers are clustered in a series, paragraph, or entire article, or when related numbers appear repeatedly in an article, figures may be used throughout to facilitate comparison: She bought 7 shares of AT&T, 3 of GM, and 20 of Microsoft.

CASUAL EXPRESSIONS. Spell out numbers in figurative expressions: I must have told him a thousand times. Thanks a million.

NEGATIVES. Use an en dash or *minus:* –15°F; The temperature hit minus 15 degrees Fahrenheit. See AGES, COMMA, DECADES, FRACTIONS, HEADLINES, LISTS, TIME, and WEIGHTS AND MEASURES.

old-boy network

OB-GYN(s). Acceptable, when clear, on second reference to obstetrician-gynecologist(s), obstetrics-gynecology, and obstetrical-gynecological.

obscenity, profanity, vulgarity. Do not use such material except in quotes and even then never gratuitously or incidentally. When use of such terms is considered essential to a story, get the approval of top editors.

LEVELS OF EXPLICITNESS. If the importance of using a suspect term over-rides the offense it may give, use it: Senator Smarsky said, "Once you're on the president's shit list, you're through."

If the actual term need not be used but we want to convey its nature explicitly, do so by using an initial letter and an appropriate number of hyphens, separated by thin spaces: "Once you're on the president's s - - - list."

If neither the word nor its nature is important to the story but an explanation is needed, use a bracketed editor's note: "Once you're on the president's [enemies] list."

If the word, its nature, and its meaning are deemed unnecessary to the story, replace the offensive term with an ellipsis: "Once you're on the president's . . . list."

occupations. Lowercase: electrical engineer Jason Watson, but First Engineer Jason Watson (a title). See TITLES OF PERSONS.

October. See DATES and MONTHS.

off base. He was off base, but an off-base remark.

off hours. She goes skiing during her off hours, but an off-hours respite.

office. Capitalize in a name; lowercase otherwise: Office of Management and Budget (the budget office, the office), the U.S. attorney's office (the office).

officer. Capitalize when used before a name as an official title: Officer Ted Hooton of the Sierra Vista police.

off-limits. An off-limits bar, but the bar was off limits.

offline. Write solid when referring to computer connections: Anna went offline to read her E-mail. Offline reader programs reduce connection charges.

off-peak (adjective)

Ohio (OH in addresses; otherwise do not abbreviate)

Ohioan

OK. OK'd, OK'ing, OK's (for verb), OKs (for plural noun). A-OK. Do not use *okay*.

Oklahoma (Okla., OK in addresses)

Oklahoman

old-boy network

old guard. Lowercase when it means any group that has long defended a cause. Capitalize when it refers to Napoleon's Imperial Guard.

Old World

Olympic Games. Summer Olympic Games, Summer Olympics, the Olympics, summer games, the games, Olympic-size pool.

onboard (adjective)

once. Do not hyphenate in such combinations as once popular method.

one of those. This construction usually leads to a plural verb: She is one of those critics who make musicians cry. **Test it by turning the sentence around:** Of the critics who make musicians cry, she is one.

one out of . . . Such expressions take a singular verb: One out of 10 cardiologists takes a holistic approach, **but** Two in five physicians favor aspirin. See RATIOS.

one person, one vote, but a one-person–one-vote election

onetime (meaning former), one-time (meaning happening once)

online. Write solid when referring to computer connections: Mabel created an online news service. Melissa went online to contact the users' bulletin board.

only. Take care, because its placement in a sentence can alter the meaning entirely, as the examples show. Generally, *only* should be as close as possible to the word it modifies:

Only I pushed the new car yesterday.
I only pushed the new car yesterday.
I pushed only the new car yesterday.
I pushed the only new car yesterday.
I pushed the new car only yesterday.
I pushed the new car yesterday only.

onstream

Ontarian. Resident of Ontario.

Ontario. Abbreviate, Ont., only in charts, maps, and tables.

onto. To a position on: He climbed onto a table, but The mayor held on to her office. Jeep moved on to Chicago.

OPEC. Acceptable on second reference to the Organization of Petroleum Exporting Countries.

op-ed. Acceptable for opposite-editorial when the meaning is clear.

operas, names of. Follow the opera's capitalization and italicize: *Tristan und Isolde*. See TITLES OF WORKS.

Operation. Capitalize in names: Operation Restore Hope, Operation Rescue.

OPI. Acceptable on second reference to overall-performance index.

or. In sentences using *or* and *nor*, the verb must agree with the noun closest to it: Neither the banks nor the government is going to back down.

oral/verbal. Oral refers to what is spoken; verbal refers to what is conveyed in words, either written or spoken.

ordinal numbers. In general, use figures for 10th and over, but spell out fractions: one tenth of the total. See FRACTIONS and NUMBERS.

Oregon (Ore., OR in addresses)

Oregonian

Oriental. Asian is generally preferred for references to people.

(-)oriented. It was a worker-oriented revolt, **but** the revolt was worker oriented.

ostmark. Lowercase references to the former East German currency.

ounce(s). Abbreviate, oz., only in charts, maps, and tables.

our, ours. See WE.

out( ). Generally solid except before capitalization: outgrow, out-Herod, **but** out-group, out-migrant, out-of-doors, out-of-pocket expenses.

over. When the meaning is clear, *over* is an acceptable alternative to *more than:* The price was over $5,000. She loaded over 16 tons of No. 9 coal. Everyone in the group was over 70. **But if** *over* **might be misread as a preposition, use** *more than* **instead:** The judge charged more than 15 officers. The shoppers picked more than 15 blouses.

over( ). Combines solid except before capitalization.

paligarchy

Pacific Rim, rim nations

Pacific states. California, Oregon, Washington, and sometimes Alaska and Hawaii. See POLITICAL REGIONS.

pact. Capitalize as part of an official name; lowercase otherwise: Warsaw Pact (the pact).

page. Capitalize with a number or letter: Page 13. Abbreviations, p., pp., are acceptable in charts and tables. See REFERENCE NOTES.

paintings. Italicize titles: *Nude Descending a Staircase.* See TITLES OF WORKS.

palate/palette/pallet. The palate is the roof of the mouth; a palette is a paint-mixing board; a pallet is a storage platform or a bed.

paligarch(s), paligarchy. Acceptable for references to a government run by a network of friends when the context makes the meaning clear.

pan(-). Combinations with lowercase words are usually written solid and lowercase: panchromatic, pandemic. Combinations with capitalized words are usually capitalized and hyphenated: Pan-Germanic, Pan-American, but Pan American Union, Panhellenic.

Panama Canal, the canal

Panama Canal treaties consist of the Panama Canal Treaty and the Treaty Concerning the Permanent Neutrality and Operation of the Panama Canal. See CANAL ZONE.

panhandle. Lowercase: the Florida panhandle, the Texas panhandle, but Panhandle, Texas (a town).

papacy

papal

paper( ). Combinations not in the dictionary usually should be two words when used as a noun, hyphenated when used as an adjective.

Pap test, Pap smear

parallel. Use figures and lowercase: 46th parallel.

parallel construction. Avoid inconsistent construction, which jars and confuses the reader.

Incorrect: Drinking late at night can cause belligerency, exhaustion, indigestion and increase absenteeism.

Correct: Drinking late at night can cause belligerency, exhaustion, and indigestion and increase absenteeism.

Better: Drinking late at night can cause belligerency, exhaustion, and indigestion. It also increases absenteeism.

Incorrect: Birkner cited three reasons for buying municipal bonds:
Long-run stability
Tax-free status
They give the holder a stake in the community.

Two of these points are things; the third is a statement. They do not fit together in a package, which makes the combination difficult to read and understand.

parentheses. Use parentheses to enclose proper-noun identifiers, certain interpolations, and reference notes: the *Clarksburg* (W.Va.) *Exponent,* but the Rehoboth Beach, Del., tournament. The tusk sold for 15 kwacha (about $38). Fifty percent of the tenants objected (box, Page 52). **For explanatory insertions, commas and dashes are less abrupt and are usually preferred to parentheses. Use brackets for editorial interpolations in quotes and for parenthetical matter within parentheses:** He said, "I will fight [the budget resolution] to the end." She approached the first senator (Jean Carnahan [left]) with the information. **Put periods outside a parenthesis at the end of a sentence if the inserted matter is part of a larger sentence, inside if the matter stands independently:** Hughlett addressed the motorcyclists (text on Page 77). Susannah was the fourth winner from her family. (A detailed list appears on Page 83.) **When a parenthetical sentence is included in another sentence, omit the first period:** The snow (she caught a glimpse of it as she passed the window) was now falling heavily. **Put caption directions in parentheses, unless the direction is the first word in a sentence:** An undercover FBI agent (left) confronts the suspect. Above, the president buys a skirt. **See PHONETIC SPELLING and REFERENCE NOTES.**

park service, but National Park Service

parliament. Capitalize when it is the actual name or the translated equivalent of a national legislative body; lowercase when it is not the actual name: British Parliament (Parliament), the Diet (Japan's parliament). A good guide to such names is the annual *Political Handbook of the World*.

parole/probation. Parole is the release on condition of good behavior of a prisoner whose sentence has not expired; probation is the suspension of a sentence of a person convicted but not yet imprisoned.

particles. When affixed to foreign names, *da, de, della, des, do, du, l', la, ten, ter, van, von,* etc., are usually kept on second reference. Do so unless you know that the individual customarily drops the particle. Keeping it is seldom incorrect in modern names. A particle repeated in a foreign surname standing alone should be capitalized or lowercased as it appears in the full name, unless it starts a sentence, when it should always be capitalized: Charles de Gaulle (de Gaulle), Ferdinand de Lesseps (de Lesseps), François de La Gorce (La Gorce), but Alexis de Tocqueville (Tocqueville).

HISTORIC NAMES should be used in their familiar forms: Johann Wolfgang von Goethe (Goethe), Hernando De Soto (De Soto), Vincent van Gogh (van Gogh), Tomás de Torquemada (Torquemada).

FOREIGN-ORIGIN NAMES. Particles are likely to be capitalized in anglicized names of foreign origin, but this is not always the case. On subsequent reference, the particle usually is capitalized or lowercased as in the full name: Paul de Kruif (a de Kruif book), Lee De Forest (the De Forest genius), James A. Van Allen (the Van Allen belt).

part-time (adjective), but working part time

part-timer

party. Capitalize in the name of a political group; lowercase alone and when *party* is not included in the name: Republican Party, Communist Party (the party), the Democratic and Republican parties, Greens Party, but Women of Russia party. Capitalize nouns and adjectives referring to membership in parties: Communist, Conservative, Republican, Green, Socialist, Laborite, Liberal, Monarchist, Know-Nothing, Nazism, Nazi. See NEW DEMOCRAT.

party designation. Except in charts and tables, avoid the parenthetical form, e.g. *(D-Md.),* in favor of such constructions as Sen. Barbara Mikulski, a Maryland Democrat. Democratic Sen. Barbara Mikulski of Maryland. Sen. Barbara Mikulski arrived. The Maryland Democrat voted yes. Sen. Barbara Mikulski headed the Maryland Democratic congressional caucus. The Democratic senators met. Maryland's Barbara Mikulski spoke.

passenger-mile

passive voice. See ACTIVE VOICE.

Passover

pastor. See entries under specific church names.

pay-per-view(s)

pay TV (noun), pay-TV (adjective)

PC. Acceptable for personal computer, politically correct, and political correctness when the meaning is clear. See POLITICALLY CORRECT.

PCP. Acceptable for the psychedelic drug phencyclidine hydrochloride when the meaning is clear.

PDT. See TIME ZONES.

peacekeeper, peacekeeping

peacemaker, peacemaking

pedal/peddle. To pedal is to propel, as on a bike; to peddle is to try to sell.

peninsula. Capitalize when part of a name; lowercase otherwise: the Iberian Peninsula (Peninsula is part of the name); the Italian peninsula (peninsula is not part of the name). See GEOGRAPHIC NAMES.

Pennsylvania (Pa., PA in addresses)

Pennsylvanian

P/E ratio. Acceptable on second reference to price-earnings ratio.

per capita. Do not hyphenate.

percent. Use figures except when the number begins a sentence. The % symbol may be used in tabular matter, headlines, and boxes: Interest was

3 percent. Prices posted an 8 percent increase. Unemployment fell only one half of 1 percent. Eighty-one percent of those replying favored Mc-Clinton. Avoid redundancies in data lists (*Percent of Americans who diet regularly: 32%*) by using words like *proportion, rate, ratio, share,* and *part* instead of *percent:* Proportion of Americans who diet regularly: 32% or Americans who diet regularly: 32%.

SUBJECT-VERB AGREEMENT. With a preposition, the verb number depends on the object of the preposition: 10 percent of the girls were; 10 percent of the class was.

MAP DATA. Use the following conventions for keys to maps:

FOR THREE CATEGORIES:	FOR FOUR CATEGORIES
less than 10%	less than 25%
10% to 50%	25% to 49%
more than 50%	50% to 74%
	75% or more

percentage point. If a rate rises from 5 percent to 6 percent, that's an increase of 1 percentage point or 1 point, not 1 percent. As a share, the increase is 20 percent.

period. Use for declarative sentences (I am well.), mildly imperative sentences (Count me out.), rhetorical questions posed as suggestions (Will you come here.), and indirect questions (She wondered why we were here.). Periods always go inside quotation marks.

TYPOGRAPHY. Use a period at the end of: notes and footnotes; sideheads that are incorporated into a line of body type; and captions, liftout quotes, and factoids that contain a complete sentence, even when the final element is not a complete sentence.

● Do not use a period at the end of: headlines and decks, even when they are a complete sentence; sideheads that appear on a separate line; table of contents entries; attributions for quotes; credits, bylines, and source lines; and captions, liftout quotes, and factoids that do not contain a complete sentence.

● Situational use. Entries in charts, tables, and boxes generally take a period when they contain a complete sentence and do not take a period when they contain only fragments. However, periods may be used with sentence fragments or not used with complete sentences for consistency within a particular chart, table, or box. Chatter in charts, tables, and boxes takes a period when it is a complete sentence. Labels end with a period when they are a sentence and with a dash, colon, ellipsis points, or no punctuation when they are not a sentence. See ABBREVIATIONS, CAPTIONS, ELLIPSIS POINTS, and INITIALS.

periodicals. See MAGAZINES, NEWSPAPERS, and TITLES OF WORKS.

periods. See AGES AND ERAS and CULTURAL DESIGNATIONS.

( )person. See GENDER BIAS.

persuade/convince. Persuade may be followed by an infinitive, but convince should never be: He was persuaded to give up his gun; she was convinced that might was right.

petty officer. See MILITARY TITLES.

phase. Prepare for Phase 1, but It was the first phase of the operation. See FAZE/PHASE.

Ph.D. (Ph.D.'s). No space between Ph. and D.

phonetic spelling. Indicate syllable stress with small caps: The composer's family name is Gajewski (pronounced guy-ESS-key).

phosphor(s) (noun). Any of various solid coatings, such as those used in television picture tubes and fluorescent bulbs, that glow when bombarded by electrons or other subatomic particles.

phosphorescence. The emission of light from an electronically excited molecule or compound.

phosphorous (adjective). Something that is of, like, or containing the element phosphorus.

phosphorus (noun). A chemical element.

physical appearance. Do not make references to a person's physical characteristics, like size, weight, color, hairstyle, imperfections, and infirmities, unless they are clearly relevant to the story. See FAIRNESS.

picket means the same as *picketer,* so use the shorter word.

pill. Lowercase when it is used in reference to birth control pills.

Place. Spell out and capitalize when part of an address. See ADDRESSES.

place names. Capitalize recognized names: the Mall (in Washington, D.C.), Lafayette Park, Lafayette and Potomac parks, Union Station, the Blue Room. See GEOGRAPHIC NAMES, GEOGRAPHIC TERMS, LOCATIONS, and the electronic PLACES list.

plains. Capitalize references to the U.S. prairie lands ranging from the Rockies to the Mississippi and North Dakota to Texas; lowercase otherwise: Great Plains, High Plains, northern Plains states, Plains Indian, but plainsman, plains grasshopper.

planes. See AIRCRAFT.

planets. See HEAVENLY BODIES.

plants, trees, flowers, and fruits. When using scientific names, capitalize the genus name, lowercase the species name, and italicize both: *Populous tremuloides.* On second reference, the genus name may be abbreviated: *P. tremuloides.* Make popular names roman, and capitalize only proper nouns and trademarks, using the dictionaries and trademark hotline (212-768-9886) for guidance: loblolly pine, black-eyed Susan, Queen of the Market aster, Golden Delicious apple.

plate. Capitalize with a number or a letter: Plate 16 (the plate).

platform. Lowercase as in the Democratic platform.

plays. Italicize titles: *Death of a Salesman.* See TITLES OF WORKS.

plea bargaining (noun), plea-bargaining (adjective)

Pledge of Allegiance, the pledge

PLO. Acceptable when clear on second reference to Palestine Liberation Organization.

plug-and-play

plurality. See MAJORITY.

plurals. CAPITALIZED TERMS. Lowercase the generic word when it is last: Yale and Harvard universities; Mississippi, Monongahela, and Ohio rivers; but the Universities of Michigan and California, Departments of State and Transportation.

FIGURES. Add *s:* 1940s, T-38s.

LETTERS. Add *s* to multiple letters (ABCs, PACs). Add *'s* to single letters (A's, p's and q's), to multiple letters with periods (Ph.D.'s), and where confusion might otherwise result (SOS's).

PROPER NAMES. When a name ends in a sibilant, add *es:* Joneses, Truaxes, Cashes. Otherwise, add *s:* the two Marys, the two Germanys, Royal Air Force Tornados, but the Rockies, the Alleghenies.

SAME SPELLING. For words whose singular and plural spellings are the same, like *corps* and *deer,* the number is determined by context and the number of the verb.

ABBREVIATED TITLES are not especially elegant in the plural, but when you must use them, add an *s:* Profs., Govs., Sens., Gens., etc.

plus. When *plus* is used as a conjunction, commas are not usually necessary, but sometimes the cadence of a sentence calls for them:

Intelligence plus luck pulled him through.
Intelligence, plus a strong element of luck, won out.
In figures: 50 million plus, but 50-plus millions, 7,000-plus mutual funds.

p.m. See TIME.

PO. Acceptable for post office in addresses: PO Box 642.

podium/lectern. A podium is a platform that a speaker stands on. A lectern is a stand that holds a speaker's notes.

poems. Quote titles of short poems. Italicize titles of poetry collections and long poems published separately. See TITLES OF WORKS and VERSE.

police titles. Capitalize official titles when they come before a name; lowercase otherwise: Officer Howard Bledsoe, Officer Bledsoe, the officer, Patrolwoman Katherine Jones. For military-style titles, follow the rules under MILITARY TITLES, preceding the title with *police* when needed for clarity.

policy is generally lowercased in names of governmental lines of action, but capitalize the surrounding words if the names are well established: the Open Door policy, an open-door policy toward Canada, America's Good Neighbor policy, a good-neighbor policy among Caribbean nations, Russia's New Economic Policy (**official name of a regulation**), George Bush's economic policy.

policymaker

policymaking

political action committee. PAC is acceptable on second reference.

political divisions. Spell out nine and below; use figures for 10 and above: Fifth Congressional District, the district; 10th Ward, the ward; 16th Precinct, the precinct.

politically correct. The term is dismissive, usually implying that the view or action it describes is oversensitive and perhaps hypocritical and unprincipled, so don't apply it to something in a news story unless the application is attributed to someone. Politically correct and political correctness may be abbreviated PC when the meaning is clear.

political movements. Lowercase political movements and beliefs not tied to a particular party as well as references to persons holding such beliefs unless the movements are derived from proper names: communism, communist (**in a philosophical sense**), Marxism, Marxist, fascism, fascist, democracy, a democracy, conservative thinking, a socialist (**in thought**), socialist tendencies, monarchist rumblings, **but** the Monarchist Party. See PARTY.

political regions. The following lists may be altered somewhat to suit particular situations, such as when an article is based on a source other than *U.S. News*'s own analysts.

EAST
> NEW ENGLAND STATES: Connecticut, Maine, Massachusetts, New Hampshire, Rhode Island, Vermont
> OTHERS: Delaware, New Jersey, New York, Pennsylvania
> BORDER: Kentucky, Maryland, Missouri, Oklahoma, West Virginia

SOUTH

DEEP SOUTH: Alabama, Georgia, Louisiana, Mississippi, South Carolina
OTHERS: Arkansas, Florida, North Carolina, Tennessee, Texas, Virginia

MIDWEST

FARM BELT STATES: Iowa, Kansas, Minnesota, Nebraska, North Dakota, South Dakota, Wisconsin
OTHERS: Illinois, Indiana, Michigan, Ohio

MOUNTAIN: Arizona, Colorado, Idaho, Montana, Nevada, New Mexico, Utah, Wyoming

FAR WEST PACIFIC STATES: California, Oregon, Washington

OTHERS: Alaska, Hawaii

(The 10 Eastern states are sometimes referred to as the North Atlantic states, Delaware, Maryland, New Jersey, New York, and Pennsylvania as the Middle Atlantic states. All five Far Western states are sometimes referred to as the Pacific states.)

political terms. Do not use quotes for those that have achieved historical significance or familiarity: New Deal, Bull Moose, Great Society, New Frontier. But take care to ensure that the terms are understood: the Bull Moose campaign of Teddy Roosevelt, Lyndon Johnson's Great Society. Use quotes with the first reference to new, ephemeral, or obscure movements or campaign slogans: "New Federalism," "Prague Spring," the "Free Doobies" movement. Some such terms should be quoted, lowercase: "new right."

politics is usually singular but sometimes plural, depending on the context: Politics is the art of the possible; Your politics make me sick.

poll. Capitalize when part of an organization's name; lowercase otherwise: Gallup Poll, Harris Poll (the poll).

pompom/pom-pom/pompon. Use pompom for cheerleader equipment, pom-pom for guns, and pompon for certain flowers.

pontiff, a pontiff, the pontiffs

pope. Capitalize before a name; lowercase otherwise: Pope John Paul II (the pope, a pope). Use titles like Holy Father and His Holiness only in direct quotes.

Portuguese names. Some surnames are single, as in Luis Martins. Some are double, as in Albino Cabral Pessoa. Double surnames put the mother's name first and the father's second. Thus if one surname is used in subsequent mention of a person, it should be the last surname. Be sure you are referring to a Portuguese, not a Spaniard; Spanish surnames place the mother's last, and it is generally a faux pas to use the mother's name alone. Most Portuguese repeat only one surname, but a few choose to repeat both if they have two: Luis Martins (Martins), João Hall Themido (Themido), Maria Soares Cordeiro (Soares Cordeiro).

possessives. See APOSTROPHE.

post(-). Follow the dictionaries (*New World,* then *Third International,* then *Random House,* then *American Heritage*): postnatal, post-mortem. For words not listed there and when *post* precedes a capital letter, use a hyphen: the post-Cold War economy, post-Watergate attitude, post-crash decisions.

post office, but U.S. Postal Service, the Postal Service

pound(s). Abbreviation, lb., is acceptable in charts, maps, and tables. See WEIGHTS AND MEASURES.

pounds per square inch. Abbreviation, psi, is acceptable on second reference and in charts, maps, and tables.

PR. Acceptable for public relations when the meaning is clear.

pre(-). Combines solid except before capitalization or an *e* or to avoid confusion: pre-eminence, pre-eminent, pre-existing, pre-judicial (before a judicial hearing), prejudicial (causing prejudice).

precinct. Capitalize in a name; lowercase alone: Sixth Precinct (the precinct).

precise words. See EXACT WORDS.

prefixes. See HYPHEN.

premier/première. Premier is a chief official, first in time, or foremost; première is a first performance or a first or leading female performer: *première danseuse.*

premier, prime minister. They have the same meaning in reference to heads of sovereign governments, but nations have traditionally used one word or the other. Use premier for the heads of government in France, China, and Taiwan; chancellor for Germany and Austria; and prime minister for most other nations. A good guide to appropriate titles is the *Political Handbook of the World* (CSA Publications).

preposition at the end of a sentence is better than an awkward phrase.

Presbyterian. Presbyterian Church (U.S.A.) is the main body of Presbyterians, organized in 1983 with the merger of the Presbyterian Church in the United States (the Southern organization) and the United Presbyterian Church in the United States of America (the Northern organization). First Presbyterian Church (the church); the Rev. Richard Rouse, pastor, First Presbyterian Church (the pastor, Rouse). Elders are elected laypersons: Karen Cleese, an elder of the Presbyterian Church (U.S.A.). The General Assembly, elected each year, is the top policymaking body. Members are called commissioners. The head of the assembly is the moderator, also elected each year. Mary Jones, a commissioner to the General Assembly (Jones); the Rev. Thomas Byers, a commissioner to the General Assembly (Byers); Geneva Roberts, moderator of the General Assembly. The highest official in the church is the General Assembly stated clerk, an elected position, which may be held by either a layperson or an ordained minister: Blaine Mueller, stated clerk of the Presbyterian Church (U.S.A.). Geographically, synods are groups of presbyteries. The Synod of the Mid-Atlantic, for instance, covers a large territory that includes the Washington, D.C., area. Each synod has a synod executive. Presbyteries are groups of congregations. The National Capital Presbytery covers the Washington area. Alternative titles for the head of a presbytery are executive presbyter and general presbyter.

presidency

president. Capitalize before a name; lowercase otherwise: President Abraham Lincoln (President Lincoln, the president, the U.S. president), company President Todd Van (the president). The first names of American presidents need not be used on first reference with the title unless confusion would otherwise result.

president, U.S. Because Grover Cleveland was both the 22nd and the 24th president of the United States, George W. Bush is the 43rd president but the 42nd to hold the office.

president-elect. Capitalize before a name; lowercase otherwise: President-elect Joseph Walsh, the president-elect.

presidential

president pro tem of the Senate. Capitalize before a name; lowercase otherwise.

priest. See ROMAN CATHOLIC CHURCH.

primary day

prime minister. See PREMIER, PRIME MINISTER.

Prince Edward Island. Use P.E.I. only in charts, maps, and tables.

Prince Edward Islander. Islander is acceptable on second reference.

prison. See JAIL.

prizes. Capitalize names, but lowercase awards representing levels of victory in track meets, fairs, etc.: the Good Conduct Medal (the medal), Legion of Merit, Pulitzer Prize for fiction (Pulitzer Prize), Silver Star, Nobel Prize in literature, Nobel Peace Prize (the peace prize), Purple Heart, Medal of Freedom, Medal of Honor, silver medal in the 100-meter dash, blue ribbon for best yearling bull. See FELLOW and SCHOLARSHIP.

pro(-). Hyphenate made-up combinations: pro-union, pro-patent.

probation. See PAROLE/PROBATION.

profanity. See OBSCENITY, PROFANITY, VULGARITY.

professor. Abbreviate and capitalize before a full name; spell out and lowercase otherwise: Prof. Paul Denzer (Professor Denzer; Denzer, an English professor; the professor), law Prof. Albert Bundy, but Paul Denzer, Edgar Allan Poe Professor of English. When qualifying words make a title more a description than a title, the title may be spelled out and lowercased: European-history professor Jill Lotto.

(-)prone. Combinations are usually hyphenated: accident-prone.

pronunciation. See ACCENTS and PHONETIC SPELLING.

( )proof. Write simple combinations solid, even if they are not in the dictionary, but hyphenate complicated inventions: rainproof, tamperproof, but indoctrination-proof.

Prop. Acceptable on second reference to Proposition when used with a number and the meaning is clear: Proposition 187, Prop. 187, the proposition.

property tax (noun), property-tax (adjective)

prophet. Capitalize when it means Mohammed: The Prophet died in 632, but the prophet Mohammed introduced Islam.

pro rata (adverb and adjective)

province. Capitalize in a name; lowercase otherwise: La Belle Province de Québec (Quebec province, the province of Quebec, the province, a province).

pseudo. Use two words for made-up combinations not in the dictionary; hyphenate when such a combination is used as an adjective: a pseudo antique, pseudo-antique chairs.

PS (public school). PS 131

P.S. (postscript)

PST. See TIME ZONES.

PTA, PTSA. Acceptable on all references to Parent-Teacher Association and Parent-Teacher-Student Association, respectively, when the meaning is clear.

publications. See MAGAZINES, NEWSPAPERS, and TITLES OF WORKS.

public-opinion poll

Puerto Rican

Puerto Rico. Use PR only in addresses; use P.R. only in charts, maps, and tables.

Pulitzer Prize, Pulitzer Prize for fiction, Pulitzer Prizes, Pulitzers. John Steinbeck won the prize for fiction in 1939.

pullout. When a pullout is an exact repetition of the wording in the body of an article, use quotation marks; when it is a paraphrase, drop the quotation marks. See QUOTATIONS.

punctuation. Use the minimum needed to promote clarity and avoid confusion. Punctuation marks generally take the font of the preceding word or character: Badham directed *Whose Life Is It Anyway?* Exceptions are parentheses and brackets when the beginning or the end of enclosed italicized material is roman: "Louis directed it [the theatrical version of *Whose Life Is It Anyway?*] in Baltimore"; question marks and exclamation marks when the marks are not part of an italicized title: Did Brooks direct *Broadcast News*?; and apostrophes in possessive constructions: It was director **Jan Sverak**'s debut. See separate entry for each punctuation mark.

P

quotation marks

Q&A

Quakers. See FRIENDS, RELIGIOUS SOCIETY OF.

quarter. Abbreviate, qtr. or q., only in charts, maps, and tables. Capitalize, Q., in table stubs. See CHARTS AND TABLES.

quarter century

quasi(-). Use two words for noun combinations; hyphenate combinations with adjectives: quasi editor, quasi-official statement.

Quebec. Abbreviate, Que., only in charts, maps, and tables.

Québécois (plural same): A French Canadian in or from Quebec province. Quebecer(s): Anybody in or from Quebec province.

queen. Capitalize before a name; lowercase otherwise. Use roman numerals: Queen Elizabeth II (the queen).

question mark. Put inside quotation marks when the question is part of the quote; otherwise put outside: "Are you going to Malibu?" Rocky asked Dennis. How can you tell if the "time is right"? See PERIOD.

quotation marks. STATEMENTS. Put quotation marks around wording quoted verbatim from an informant, speaker, document, book, magazine article, or similar source. Do not place marks around material that has been paraphrased or altered in any way except by nonsubstantive style changes or by deletions indicated with ellipsis points or by explanatory matter inserted between brackets. Complete texts or lengthy excerpts appearing as separate features or boxes sometimes go without quotation marks, but they must be properly introduced to make their origin clear.

TITLES

ROMAN TYPE AND QUOTATION MARKS

articles	monographs
booklets	pamphlets
chapters	reports
dissertations	short poems
episodes of radio and tv programs	short stories
essays	songs
headlines	speeches
lectures	theses

ITALIC TYPE, NO QUOTATION MARKS
almanacs
ballets
books
comic books
comic strips
dictionaries
encyclopedias
magazines
movies
musical compositions (long) with distinctive names
newsletters
newspapers
operas
oratorios
paintings
periodicals
photographs
plays
poems (long) published separately
poetry collections
radio series
sculpture
television series

ROMAN TYPE, NO QUOTATION MARKS
computer operating systems
religious books, like the Bible and the Koran
word-processing programs

PARTIAL SENTENCES beginning a quote may lead directly into a continuation of the quote: Brown said that the building "is a monstrosity. It should be torn down and replaced."

PUNCTUATION. Commas and periods always come before a close quote, even if they have nothing to do with the matter quoted: Senator Wenta said he had not read "Tilly's Tale," but Morris has read it twice. Senator Sullivan still votes with Senator Flinchum, even though she has referred to him as a "bunco artist." Semicolons go outside quotation marks. Colons, exclamation points, and question marks are placed inside quotation marks when part of the quotation; otherwise they are outside: One question the president kept asking himself: Who were these "cronies"?
He demanded, "Who are they?"
Hughlett said, "Jail the thieves"; Carson put them away.
Zappardino had this to say about "sly embezzlers": They slink.

YES AND NO. Quote when capitalized; no quotes when lowercase:
I say yes. You say no.
I say "Yes." You say "No."

SINGLE QUOTES. Use single quotes in headlines; decks; quotations within quotations; subheads on a line of their own; and drop initial caps. Use double quotes in precedes, captions, sideheads, liftout quotes, and body type. All-cap heads integrated with body type are considered headlines and so take single quotes.

MISCELLANEOUS. Do not use quotation marks around slang, designations of political faith, or names of buildings, homes, ships, boats, or planes. See ACCENTS; ITALICS; LOCATIONS; NICKNAMES; SIGNS; SLANG, DIALECT, AND JARGON; TITLES OF WORKS; and ( ) WORD.

quotations. We use two main kinds of quotations: (1) Language from printed articles, documents, letters, and similar records, including recorded *USN&WR* interviews. (2) Language attributed to others in reporters' memories or notes. These two kinds require a shade of difference in treatment.

WHEN LANGUAGE IS ON THE RECORD, we make no changes beyond those required by printing style, such as spelling or capitalizing words our way or moving commas from a position after quotation marks to before—and even here, we have to be careful if there is a danger of altering the meaning. If we leave anything out, we must indicate a deletion. To condense or otherwise change a statement so that it sounds better in our context—unless we have the writer's permission—is beyond our province; the only way to make such changes is to paraphrase, outside quotation marks.

IN QUOTATIONS FROM MEMORY or from notes taken on the scene, it is up to a reporter to tell what the person said, not what the reporter thinks the person meant to say or ought to have said. If the quote does not make sense as spoken, the only solution is to give up the quote or query the person quoted. Details such as punctuation are the duty of the reporter and the editors, who must place commas and periods in such a way as to give the most accurate account of what was spoken.

BLIND QUOTES occur when someone is giving us sensitive information and requests anonymity. Sometimes there is no alternative but to use them. But a habit has grown up in modern political writing of using blind quotes as a crutch or as a version of the old Greek chorus (*"Cheney looked old today," a longtime associate said*). Cut such quotes wherever possible. A blind quote should stay in if the material is intrinsically interesting or if there is some compelling reason for keeping the speaker's identity secret. But when you find yourself writing, *"The future lies ahead," one observer noted,* then just cut the blind quote and make the point yourself.

PRONUNCIATION is largely in the ear of the hearer. It is hard to prove how somebody spoke, and, in any case, doubt always remains as to whose pronunciation is correct. To call attention to pronunciation by misspelling a word is often to ridicule the speaker.

A SPEAKER'S GRAMMAR is the speaker's own and should not routinely be cleaned up to meet our own publishing standards. Even a college professor should not be made to talk as if at a lecture. If the professor told us, "I don't know who we ought to hire," we should let the professor say it that way and not change the *who* to *whom*.

LIFTOUT QUOTES. When a quotation is pulled from a story and set in large type, put a period at the end if the quote is a complete sentence. When a liftout consisting of words written by us, as in an editorial or a column, varies from the wording in the article itself, drop the quotation marks.

Q

revolutions per minute

racial designations. Do not use racial or ethnic designations unless they are essential to the story. See (-)AMERICAN, ASIAN, BLACK, CHICANO, COLORED, HISPANIC, LATINO, and NEGRO.

rack/wrack. As a noun, use rack to mean a framework; as a verb, use it to mean to spread out, torture, trouble, torment, or score: The suspect was tortured on the rack. She racked her brain. The suspense was nerve-racking. She racked up 15 straight points. Use wrack, as a noun, to mean ruin or destruction; as a verb, use it to mean to ruin or destroy: wrack and ruin; The car was wracked up by the train.

radio. Use italics for names of series. Make names of episodes roman with quotes: *The Rush Limbaugh Show,* "Baba Booey Gets Caught."

railroad, railway. Spell out and capitalize as part of a name; lowercase alone. Note that Rail Road is two words in some names.

railroad abbreviations. Use an ampersand, no periods, no spaces: B&O.

R&D. Acceptable on second reference to research and development.

ranges. When referring to a range of time or price in parentheses or in a box, use an en dash (open March–November, 3 p.m.–9 p.m., seats priced $14–$37), but in regular text, use *to* or *through.* See PERCENT.

rank and file, a rank-and-file decision

rathole

ratios. Use figures: She reported that 3 of every 4 Californians support Proposition 19; the ratio was 2 to 1, a 2-to-1 ratio. But when the first number is spelled out, as at the beginning of a sentence, spell out the second number as well if it is less than 10: One in three Americans believes Satan is real.

raw material (noun), raw-material (adjective)

RBI(s). Acceptable for run(s) batted in when clear.

re(-). Write solid except before an *e* or capitalization, or in confusing combinations: re-cover (to cover anew), re-form (to form again), re-create (to create again).

(-)ready. Usually hyphenated in combinations: a combat-ready platoon, but the platoon was combat ready, combat readiness.

real estate (noun), real-estate (adjective)

Realtor is a trademark. Use only for members of the National Association of Realtors. Generic equivalents are real-estate broker, real-estate agent, real-estate specialist.

recision/rescission. Use recision to mean a cutting back; use rescission to mean a rescinding or a nullification: lower sales forced a recision in research and development (the outlay for research and development was reduced); the rescission bill revoked $12 billion in defense spending authority (the authority was rescinded, which resulted in a reduction—a recision—in spending); the court ordered a rescission of the merger agreement (the merger was annulled).

recordings. See MUSICAL COMPOSITIONS and TITLES OF WORKS.

Red. Do not use as a synonym for Communist. If it appears that way in a quotation or in a historical context, capitalize it.

reference books, titles of. Use italics: *Encyclopedia Americana, Encyclopedia of Beach Volleyball, Webster's New World College Dictionary, World Almanac.* See BOOK TITLES and TITLES OF WORKS.

reference notes. Use parentheses: (box on Page 80) or (box, Page 80). Avoid language like *(see box, Page 80)* that suggests we are ordering readers about.

regiment. Capitalize in a name; lowercase alone: 5th Regiment, 41st Regiment, the regiment.

regions. See NATIONS AND REGIONS and POLITICAL REGIONS.

Regular Army

reign/rein. Reign is to rule or prevail; rein is to restrain or guide.

religious denominations. Capitalize official and shortened names; lowercase *church* by itself: the Roman Catholic Church (the Catholic Church, the church), the Episcopal Church (the church). See CHURCH, DENOMINATIONS, and separate entries for specific denominations.

religious personages. Capitalize personages in religious lore and history: the Baptist, the Blessed Virgin, Buddha, Messiah, Mother of God, the Prophet (meaning Mohammed), Queen of Heaven, the Virgin, the Virgin Mary, Holy Father. See DEITY and POPE.

Religious Society of Friends. See FRIENDS, RELIGIOUS SOCIETY OF.

Rep. Abbreviate when used before a complete name as a legislative title (Rep. Tina Kasparowitz, state Rep. Jamal Konkus). Spell out when used with a last name (Representative Kasparowitz). Spell out and lowercase otherwise (the representative). Avoid using the abbreviation in situations where it might be confused with Republican. See CONGRESSPERSON.

repetition. Avoid undue repetition of a word or phrase, which can distract readers or turn them off. At the same time, realize that in some situations repetition is acceptable and even desirable or necessary, and beware of avoidance techniques whose cure is worse than the disease.

representative at large. Rep. at Large Henry Lewis, the representative at large, a representative-at-large election.

republic. Capitalize when part of a name; lowercase otherwise: Dominican Republic (the republic), Republic of Namibia.

Republican. Abbreviate, Rep. or R, but only in charts, maps, and tables and then only when it will not be confused with representative.

Republican national chairman. Capitalize before a name; lowercase otherwise: Republican National Chairman Clyde Backhaus (the Republican national chairman).

Republican National Committee, the committee

Republican National Convention, the national convention, the Republican convention, the GOP convention

Republican Party, Republicans, the party, the GOP

Reserve(s). Capitalize for a specific military group; lowercase for members. See ARMY RESERVE, NAVAL RESERVE, etc.

Reserve Officers Training Corps (ROTC)

resister/resistor. A resister is someone who resists or something that resists; a resistor is an electrical device.

restrictive clauses. See THAT, WHICH.

resurrection. Capitalize references to the biblical event; lowercase otherwise: The Resurrection is celebrated on Easter; Gerstung's political resurrection was fast and brief.

retired. Abbreviate in parentheses when used after a name: Lt. Gen. Bernard Grady, USA (Ret.); Rear Adm. Doug Yerkes, USN (Ret.).

Reuters. The name of the company and, since 1997, the spelling to use for photo and story credits.

reverend, the (the Rev.). Abbreviate before a full name; spell out otherwise: the Rev. Willy Wirtz; on second reference, Wirtz. Do not use Reverend, Rev., or the Rev. with the last name only. Avoid the colloquial *reverend* as a noun except in quotations. The *the* may be dropped in headlines, charts, tables, and letters-to-the-editor signatures and to follow an individual's preference. Do not use double titles, such as *the Rev. Dr. Arberg.* See TITLES OF PERSONS and entries for specific denominations.

revolution. Capitalize historical names: the French Revolution, the American Revolution. Capitalize Revolutionary War and the Revolution when referring to the American Revolution. Lowercase revolution standing alone when it refers to something other than the American Revolution. Lowercase plural constructions: the French and American revolutions.

revolutions per minute. rpm is acceptable on all references when the meaning is clear.

Rhode Island (R.I., RI in addresses)

Rhode Islander

Rhodes scholar. See SCHOLARSHIP.

riffle/rifle. Riffle is to leaf rapidly through; rifle is to ransack or pillage.

right. Lowercase unless it is part of the official name of a political party: the right wing of the party, a right-wing caucus. Don't use *right-winger* except in quoted matter.

right of way, right-of-way contract

right-to-life. See ABORTION-DEBATE TERMINOLOGY.

riven. Past participle of *rive*.

river. Capitalize as part of a name; lowercase alone: Red River (the river), the Mississippi and Missouri rivers.

Road. Spell out and capitalize in an address. See ADDRESSES.

rockets. For names not listed here, consult *Jane's All the World's Aircraft* and *Jane's Weapon Systems,* but make all figures arabic regardless of *Jane's* usage.

U.S. ROCKETS and rocket stages generally are known by popular names, which sometimes are followed by numerals that stand for model numbers: Titan 3, Saturn 5, Minuteman 3, Titan 3D, S-4B (rocket stage). Submarine-launched missiles are known by their names, sometimes followed by letters and numbers: Polaris A-2, Poseidon C-3, Polaris A-3, Trident 1.

RUSSIAN ROCKETS. SS-4, SS-9, SS-14. Surface-to-air (antiaircraft) missiles are designated by SA and number: SA-3. Most of these missiles have been given names, but they are usually known by letter and number.

role/roll. A role is a part or a character; a roll is a membership list or a bun.

roll call, roll-call vote

rollover (noun and adjective)

Roman Catholic Church. the Catholic Church, St. James's Roman Catholic Church (the church, a Roman Catholic church, a Roman Catholic), the Rev. Xavier Moore, pastor of St. James's Roman Catholic Church (the pastor, Father Moore, the priest, Moore). Priest is a proper vocational description for ordained men from a pastor up to and including the pope. Bishop Xavier Proctor of Atlanta (Bishop Proctor, the bishop, Proctor), Cardinal Xavier Cook (Cardinal Cook, the cardinal, Cook), Pope Leo XIII (Pope Leo, Leo, the pope, a pope), Msgr. Thomas Cox (Monsignor Cox, the monsignor, Cox). Monsignor is an honorary title conferred by the pope on some priests who are not bishops. Do not use two titles: *the Rev. Msgr. Xavier O'Donnell.* The Very Rev. and the Most Rev. are used in referring to the superiors general of some Roman Catholic orders.

SACRAMENTS of the Roman Catholic Church, some of which are shared by other denominations:

anointing of the sick, essentially the rite formerly called extreme unction. Say "administered last rites" if that is what they were, or "administered the sacrament of anointing" to the person.
baptism
confirmation
Eucharist, eucharistic; Holy Communion, Communion, also in some denominations the Lord's Supper
holy orders (ordination ceremonies of the priesthood)
matrimony (the marriage ceremony)
reconciliation (penance)

roman numerals. See NUMBERS.

roman type

room. Capitalize in a name or with a number or a letter: East Room, the Lincoln Bedroom, Room 320, Room 3A.

ROTC. Acceptable on first reference to Reserve Officers Training Corps if context makes the meaning clear.

round. Round 12, Round 4, 12th round, fourth round, 12th-round knockout.

route. See HIGHWAY NAMES.

royalty. Princes and princesses are "royal highnesses"; reigning monarchs are "majesties." Use such terms only when quoting someone. See YOUR HONOR.

R.R. Use for Railroad only in charts, maps, and tables.

Rt. Rev. Always abbreviate when used as a title before a name.

run-up (noun)

Russian. Do not use for references to non-Russian citizens of the former Soviet Union or of the Commonwealth of Independent States. For references to individuals and specific groups, use the applicable national term, such as Russians, Georgians, Armenians, or Ukrainians.

Russian names. Follow the spellings of individuals who have made their preferences known, then use the electronic NAMES list, then *Webster's New World College Dictionary,* then *Webster's Biographical Dictionary.* For names that are in the news but have not yet made it into one of the above sources, current newspaper spellings are acceptable. If no other guide is available, follow these rules of thumb:

1. Do not use diacritical marks.
2. Spell names beginning with a *ye* sound *ye,* not *e:* Yevgeni, not *Evgeni;* Yekaterina, not *Ekaterina.* But Eduard (the sound is *e*).
3. Use *yo,* not *e,* for the *yo* sound: Pyotr, not *Petr.*
4. In general, use the ending *i* rather than *y, iy, yi, yj, ii, ij* for first and last names: Dmitri, not *Dmitriy;* Yuri, not *Yuriy;* for the feminine ending in first names, use ia, not *iya* or *iia:* Viktoria, not *Viktoriya;* Maria, not *Marya.*
5. Do not anglicize spellings for the sake of it. Viktor and Aleksandr, for example, are both acceptable, but bear in mind that historical usage or individual preference may dictate Victor and Alexander.
6. Use the feminine ending in a last name if the woman has an independent reputation; otherwise keep the masculine ending: Anna Pavlova, not *Pavlov,* but Raisa Gorbachev, not *Gorbacheva.*

R

sacraments. Capitalize Eucharist, Holy Communion, Communion, Lord's Supper. Lowercase anointing of the sick, baptism, confirmation, holy orders, matrimony, sacrament of reconciliation, mass, high mass, low mass, requiem mass.

Saint, Sainte, Saints (St., Ste., SS.). Use the abbreviations for all saints, geographical names, and organizations. Alphabetize as they appear, letter by letter, ignoring word spaces, hyphens, dashes, virgules, and apostrophes:

SS. Peter and Paul Church
St. Andrews Presbyterian College
Stanford University
St. Anselm College

Saskatchewan. Abbreviate, Sask., only in charts, maps, and tables.

Saskatchewanian

SAT. Before March 1994, it stood for Scholastic Aptitude Test, which was replaced by SAT I: Reasoning Test. What were known prior to March 1994 as Achievement Tests are now SAT II: Subject Tests. SAT I and SAT II are now collectively known as the Scholastic Assessment Tests.

Satan. Capitalize Devil when it means Satan, but lowercase devils, a devil.

satellites. See SPACE VEHICLES.

savings and loan association. Use an ampersand in abbreviations and in official names: S&L, S&Ls, Nickerson Savings & Loan Association, the savings and loan.

savings bonds, U.S. savings bonds

say is the all-purpose neutral verb of attribution. Exercise care when using others, which can carry additional meaning:

● state adds formality.
● declare and proclaim add formality or openness or imply an official announcement.
● assert is to say confidently.
● allege is to assert, especially without proof.
● indicate and suggest add a tentative or indirect quality.
● maintain implies defensiveness.

- claim may imply that the writer has reason to disbelieve what was said. A more neutral alternative is assert.
- note, affirm, and point out imply that what is said is demonstrably true. Use them only when dealing with facts, not opinions, claims, or speculation.
- disclose and reveal imply past concealment.
- admit implies shame or confession.
- laugh, chuckle, snort, muse, etc., are generally amateurish and should be used sparingly, if at all. See CLAIM.

Scandinavian countries. Norway, Sweden, and Denmark. Iceland and the Faeroe Islands are sometimes included, as is Finland, but Finland is related by language to Estonia and Hungary rather than to Scandinavia.

scene. Capitalize with a number; lowercase alone: Scene 1 (the scene).

schedule. Capitalize with a number or a letter; lowercase alone: Schedule D, Schedule 25 (the schedule).

schizophrenic (adjective). Avoid using as a noun, which emphasizes a disability at the expense of the person's individuality.

scholar. Lowercase as in Rhodes scholar.

scholarship. Capitalize in the name of an award; lowercase alone: a Rhodes Scholarship (the scholarship, a Rhodes scholar).

school. See COLLEGES AND UNIVERSITIES.

school subjects. Capitalize names of specific courses and proper nouns; lowercase otherwise: Literature II, Journalism 202, Fundamentals of Biology, Latin, Greek, English history, mathematics, calculus. See COURSE TITLES.

scientific names. See GENUS AND SPECIES.

scores. Use figures.

S corporation

Scotch (adjective). In general, use Scotch when referring to things (Scotch whisky), Scottish when referring to people (Scottish voters).

Scotch whisky, but whiskey for generic references. See WHISKEY.

Scripture. See BIBLICAL REFERENCES.

SEAL(s). Nickname for members of the sea, air, and land forces of the Naval Special Warfare Command.

seasons. Lowercase unless they are personified: the spring of 1977; when Autumn came on in her bright bangles.

second(s). Abbreviate, sec., only in charts, maps, and tables. Spell out below 10; use figures above nine. See NUMBERS.

Second, the. In names, use roman numerals, no commas: King William II, Mario Arble II. Do not use unless an individual is known that way or it is necessary to distinguish one person from another. See NUMBERS.

secretary. Capitalize when part of a formal title before a name; lowercase otherwise: Secretary of State Gil Shawk (the secretary of state).

secretary general. Capitalize before a name; lowercase otherwise: U.N. Secretary General Kerry Kelly (Secretary General Kelly, the secretary general).

sect. Definitions vary, but since the word is generally regarded as disparaging, don't use it in reference to a particular group in a news story unless the word is attributed to someone.

section. Capitalize with a number or letter; lowercase otherwise: Section 2, the second section, the section.

Security Council (of the United Nations), the council

see. See REFERENCE NOTES.

self(-). Hyphenate made-up combinations.

semi( ). Write combinations solid except before a capital letter or an *i*.

semiautomatic/automatic weapons. A semiautomatic fires once and reloads each time the trigger is pulled. An automatic fires as long as the trigger is held or until the ammunition is exhausted. See FIREARMS.

semicolon. It is useful where a somewhat more authoritative stop than a comma is needed. Place semicolons outside quotation marks.

IN A COMPOUND SENTENCE, a semicolon can provide a pleasing balance: Tad played faster; Crystal worked harder. Semicolons in this type of sentence can add interest and variety to copy. Overuse, however, can produce a formal style that reads like an essay. Avoid merely stringing ideas together with semicolons when their relationship needs more explanation.

DIVISIONS BETWEEN PHRASES that already have commas should be made with semicolons: They chose cattle wrangling, snipe hunting, and plinking in Wyoming; bird-watching in Canada and Greece; volleyball in Florida; and salmon fishing in Scotland.

Senate. Capitalize references to the U.S. Senate or to a legislative body of a state or a foreign country if that is the name it uses. Abbreviate, Sen., only in charts, maps, and tables.

senator. Capitalize and abbreviate before a full name; spell out with last name only; lowercase otherwise: Sen. Bruno Moore (Senator Moore, the senator), a senator, two senators. See PARTY DESIGNATIONS.

senatorial

sentence fragments. Favored by automobile-advertisement copywriters, sentence fragments in news copy are almost always too precious. And difficult to understand. Which is why they should be used rarely. If at all.

sentence length. A mixture of short and long sentences, with a variety of constructions, will help keep the reader interested and alert. Sudden insertion of a short, blunt sentence achieves emphasis. No sentence should be so long that the reader loses track of the beginning before reaching the end; re-examination of an article frequently turns up a sentence or two of this kind. A succession of one-sentence paragraphs, favored by some writers, does not necessarily help clarity; it may have the opposite effect because the reader is left to puzzle out what is related to what and how. Newsmagazine paragraphs should be reasonably short, it is true, but with each paragraph organized around a topic. An exception is a collection of single-sentence paragraphs in a series introduced by a colon or a dash.

sentence rhythm. A simple way to check the rhythm and grace of a sentence is to read it aloud and see whether its final syllable is naturally stressed. Not every sentence can end this way. (For example, the preceding one, whose final natural stress falls two words from the close.) But many of them can. (Like the preceding one.) There are endless variations—sentences that are stronger when they end with two stresses, like this. Or sentences with a penultimate or antepenultimate stress, like this one that ends with the word *ultimate*. Regardless of these variations, the points are two. First, it is worth going out of your way to be conscious of where the stress lies. Second, as a rule the higher the proportion of final-stress sentences, the smoother and more forceful the writing will seem to the reader—and the reader won't even know why.

September. See DATES and MONTHS.

series. series E savings bonds, series EE, series H, series HH.

service. Capitalize in a name; lowercase otherwise: Internal Revenue Service (the revenue service, the service).

set-aside (noun)

settlement/verdict/judgment. A settlement, which is "reached" or "agreed to," is a voluntary agreement by both sides in a civil trial. A verdict is rendered by a judge or a jury, and it can result in a judgment, which is "awarded" by the court.

set-to (noun)

sexism. See GENDER BIAS, HE/SHE, and MAN.

she, her. Do not use for countries, ships, hurricanes, or tropical storms.

sheik. Capitalize before a name; lowercase alone.

ships, names of. Capitalize, roman, no quotes. Use it, not *she.*

Shiva

shootdown (noun)

short stories. Quote titles. See TITLES OF WORKS.

[*sic*]. Confine its use to typographical errors or serious mistakes in usage that we have left in quoted material. Do not use merely to call attention to someone's incorrect grammar. Set it in italics and brackets with no period: She wrote that her husband "was unphased [*sic*] by the allegations." See QUOTATIONS.

( )sick. Usually combines solid: heartsick.

( ) side. the B side.

sign off (verb), **sign-off** (noun)

signs. In some cases, small caps, with no quotation marks, are appropriate for body-type references to signs and headlines: Virginia's sign said WE LOVE SMILEY WILLIAMS. When not using small caps, enclose sign text and headlines in quotation marks.

(-)size. Hyphenate combinations except those with a prefix that normally forms one word: whale-size, midsize. Follow the dictionary on spelling: oversize, middle-sized, undersized. For words not in the dictionary, use *-size:* full-size, family-size. When used in the predicate, drop the hyphen: The pizza was family size.

size up (verb), **size-up** (noun)

slang, dialect, and jargon. Slang and other nonstandard words create an on-the-scene ambience. They sound best in quotations from others, but we can use them to advantage in our own writing if we do it well. The absolute element is clarity to all readers. Nonstandard words are often understood only in certain regions or trades or by limited social, ethnic, or age groups. Therefore, if we use such a word we have to make sure, by context or by subtle explanation, that the meaning is plain. Do not use quotation marks around nonstandard words unless the intention is to attribute them to individuals or groups identified or implied in the copy. If we have to apologize for a word, we should not write it. Use *Webster's New World College Dictionary* as a guide to distinguishing nonstandard words by such terms as slang, colloquial, and regional.

Slovak. See CZECH, CZECHOSLOVAK.

slugs. Take care to make file names precise and consistent in all the places they appear: in the lineup, in the flowchart, in the slug itself, and, thus, in the online version's URL. For recurring features using the issue date, make the slug, for instance, 7pol, not 07pol. Do not use interior spaces or ampersands. Avoid slugs that are unseemly or that we would otherwise not want to have appear in the magazine.

small-business man, small-business woman, small-business executive, small-business investment company. See BUSINESSMAN, BUSINESS-WOMAN, and GENDER BIAS.

small caps. Small caps are used to reduce the jarring impact of capitalized abbreviations (NATO, HMO). When a possessive or a plural is used, make the *s* regular lowercase (NATO's, HMOs). Use the small-cap format for numbers that are part of small-cap abbreviations: B2B. When an abbreviation starts a sentence, put all the letters in small caps: NASA approved the flight. Do not use bold or italic type in the small-cap lead-ins in letters to the editor.

EXCEPTIONS. In general, do not use small caps in headlines or other display type; in italic type; in most boxed sans-serif type; in captions that require special coding; and with abbreviations that contain a single capital letter ("L" Class, F-18, T-shirt) or points (U.S.). When juxtaposition of abbreviations calling for small caps with those calling for regular caps creates a jarring inconsistency, all such abbreviations in a particular section of copy may be put in small caps: movies rated PG-13, R, and NC-17; World War I and World War II.

HEADLINES. When headlines are reprinted, small caps, without quotation marks, may be used for effect. But in letters to the editor, write article titles up-style in caps and lowercase, with quotation marks.

SMALL CAPS	REGULAR CAPS
AT&T	Pfc.
F/A-18	3M
CD-ROM	F-18
START II	Ph.D.
CNN	the "F" word
B&B	3-D
PCs	U.S.
MD (Postal Service	Md.
DC abbreviations)	D.C.
GOP	T-shirt
C-SPAN	*TV Guide*
TV	A in math

SMALL CAPS	REGULAR CAPS
130MHz	A.D.
NAACP-sponsored	B.C.
Super Bowl XXXIII	
P/E ratio	
Y2K	
B2B	
OK'd	
CO_2	
AGM-130	
WebMD	

smokescreen

snowbike, snowbiking, snowbiker

S.O.B.('s). Use only when quoting someone. Don't use when someone in fact said "son of a bitch." See OBSCENITY, PROFANITY, VULGARITY.

so-called (adjective), so called (adverb). Use either quotation marks or so-called; don't use both.

Social Security. Capitalize in reference to the U.S. system; lowercase generic references: your Social Security number, social security systems in Europe.

Society. Capitalize in a name; lowercase otherwise: Philadelphia Savings Fund Society (the society), high society.

software. See COMPUTER TOOLS.

someday/some day. Someday means an indefinite time in the future: I'll see Mary Louise someday, but some day in June, on some day that I'll tell you later.

someplace/some place. I left it someplace, but He is moving to some place in Arkansas.

( )something. Use figures and hyphens: 20-something, 40-somethings. As an adjective, a shorter alternative is 20-ish.

sometime/some time. Adverb (at some time not known or specified): It will happen sometime. Adjective (former, occasional): a sometime coworker. But when it means a certain or indefinite period: It happened some time ago.

song titles. Set roman, with quotation marks: "Here Comes the Sun." See MUSICAL COMPOSITIONS.

SOS('s)

sound bite

soundboard/sound board. A soundboard is a resonator in a musical instrument; a sound board, also called a sound card, is a computer part.

source lines. Most charts, maps, and tables have source lines. Set them in caps and lowercase. If more than one source is listed, separate them by commas unless semicolons are necessary for clarity. Use Dept. and Depts. for federal cabinet agencies. Otherwise, give the complete name of the agency, and avoid abbreviations that would not be used in body copy. Follow general style for italics, quotation marks, and accents:

Sources: U.S. Depts. of Labor, Commerce; estimates by *USN&WR*
Sources: U.S. Treasury Dept., *National Geographic*
Source: Federal Communications Commission

Avoid complete sentences in source lines, and do not use a period at the end. The art department indicates the position of the source line for the chart or table on its layout. Source lines for boxed charts usually run inside the rules or on the color panel that defines the borders of the box. Sometimes source lines are placed outside the apparent boundaries of charts. See CAPTIONS and CHARTS AND TABLES.

sources. Such phrases as *officials said, observers said, experts said,* and *a spokesman said* are evasive. They can leave the general reader vaguely unsatisfied and the insider suspecting that the officials are a doorman, the observers are a bartender, the experts are our reporter, and the spokesman is the third vice president's secretary. We must get as close as possible to naming real persons while remaining within the source's guidelines for attribution. Sample lines of retreat:

FOR OFFICIALS
Secretary of Agriculture Dara Lin
a top official in the Department of Agriculture
an official who has studied the agreement
an Agriculture official
a federal official **or** an official in Washington

FOR OBSERVERS
British Ambassador Joan Meredith
a Western ambassador who is a veteran in the Middle Eastern service
a veteran diplomat
a Western diplomat on the scene
an old hand in the Middle East

See EXPERT.

south, southern. Capitalize in a name or when designating the southern United States; lowercase when merely indicating a direction: the South, the Deep South, Southerner, Southern states, South Pole, the Southwest (United States), Southern Hemisphere, South Side (of Chicago), South Africa, but southern Africa, southern New Jersey, They headed south. See COMPASS DIRECTIONS, POLITICAL REGIONS, and the PLACES electronic file.

South Carolina (S.C.; SC in addresses)

South Carolinian

South Dakota (S.D.; SD in addresses)

South Dakotan

Soviet. Capitalize in references to the former Soviet Union and in names; lowercase when used alone to refer to governmental bodies: Soviet government, Soviet citizens, Soviet cars, the village soviet sent its five-year plan to the Supreme Soviet.

Soviets. Capitalize references to what was the government of the U.S.S.R. and to its people: In 1990, the Soviets offered tractors for wheat.

space age. See AGES AND ERAS.

space vehicles. Capitalize names of vehicles, satellites, and missions. Lowercase descriptive terms. Use arabic numerals: space shuttle Atlantis, Zarya, Unity, international space station, Mir space station, Viking 2, Pioneer 11, Cosmos 629, Sputnik 1, a sputnik, space buggy, moon rover, Lunokhod 1, Intelsat 4, Hubble Space Telescope (the space telescope).

Spanish-language names. The only safe guide to Spanish-language names is the way the individuals use them. Surnames are usually double, the father's (patronymic) first, the mother's (matronymic) last. Joaquín Prado Fernández on second reference would be Prado Fernández or Prado, not *Fernández*. Some double names derive from one person alone when the person has achieved fame. Spain's former prime minister, Leopoldo Calvo Sotelo, is a nephew of José Calvo Sotelo, whose assassination touched off the Spanish Civil War. He is Calvo Sotelo on second reference. Former Mexican President José López Portillo's double surname derives from his grandfather. Sometimes what looks like a double surname is not. Carlos Andrés Pérez of Venezuela uses only his patronymic. Andrés is a given name. Sometimes given names are compounds. María de los Angeles Moreno Uriegas is Moreno on second reference. Sometimes the surname is a compound. Former Mexican President Carlos Salinas de Gortari is usually referred to as Salinas on second reference. But former United Nations Secretary General Javier Pérez de Cuéllar is Pérez de Cuéllar on second reference.

GENERAL RULES
1. Use a name as the individual uses it or as it is used locally.
2. On second reference, use the first surname unless you know that the individual uses both surnames.
3. Avoid using the second surname alone. However, certain well-known individuals with common surnames are referred to by their matronymic. The poet Federico García Lorca is called Lorca or García Lorca, never *García,* which is the Smith of the Spanish language. Some persons with common surnames add the initial of the matronymic: Enrique González R. This looks odd to American eyes and should be used only if there is real doubt about which González is meant.

WOMEN'S NAMES. If María Pérez marries José González and takes her husband's name, she becomes María Pérez de González; on second reference, González.

spartan. Lowercase references to people or things characterized by self-discipline, self-denial, or frugality (spartan accommodations); capitalize references to ancient Sparta (Spartan politics).

Speaker. Capitalize as a title before a name; lowercase alone: Speaker of the House Lily Myers (Speaker Myers, the speaker), speakership.

Specialist. See MILITARY TITLES.

special prosecutor. See INDEPENDENT COUNSEL.

speeches. Use quotation marks. Capitalize principal words and prepositions and conjunctions of more than three letters: "I Have a Dream" speech, but State of the Union address.

spelling. Use the following guides in this order:
1. This stylebook, including the electronic names and places word lists.
2. The preferred entry given in *Webster's New World College Dictionary, Fourth Edition* (Macmillan). The preferred entry is taken to mean the one first mentioned; however, when the dictionary specifies "usually" with an alternative spelling for a particular definition, use that spelling.
3. *Webster's Third New International Dictionary* (G.&C. Merriam Co.).
4. *Random House Unabridged Dictionary* (Random House). See BRITISH SPELLINGS, GEOGRAPHIC NAMES, RUSSIAN NAMES, SPANISH-LANGUAGE NAMES, etc.

split infinitive. Don't hesitate to split an infinitive when doing so makes for easier reading or better understanding: . . . to boldly go where no person has gone before.

split-level (noun and adjective)

spokesperson. See GENDER BIAS.

sport/sports (adjective). sports car, sports clothes, sports medicine, sports editor, sports section, but sport coat, sport utility vehicle, sport fish, sport shirt.

Sputnik. Capitalize only in the name of an individual satellite: Sputnik 1 (the sputnik, a sputnik). See SPACE VEHICLES.

spymaster

Square. Spell out and capitalize in a name or an address; lowercase alone.

Sr. Do not set off with commas: H. Ralph Nickerson Sr. came home.

St. See SAINT, SAINTE, SAINTS.

stage directions. Italicize them and enclose them in roman brackets: Robyn: Lennon and McCartney might have been a bit more talented than we are [*laughs*].

stanch/staunch. Stanch means to stop the flow; staunch means steadfast or loyal.

standard model. Use quotation marks on first reference to the prevailing theory of the universe.

stars. See HEAVENLY BODIES.

Star-Spangled Banner, The. Put it in quotation marks, but the national anthem.

start-up (noun and adjective), start up (verb)

state. Lowercase when referring to one or more states of the United States: a state, the state, Colorado state Sen. Ashley Jones, the state Capitol. Capitalize in names: State Produce Inc., New York State, the Empire State, Washington State, the State of Israel, but the state of Washington, the state of Maryland. When a city and state are used adjectivally in a proper name, put the state in parentheses: They found the Radford (Va.) University student at home. Or consider rewriting: They found the student from Virginia's Radford University at home. See STATES.

Statehouse. Capitalize references to a specific statehouse: the Mississippi Statehouse (the Statehouse), but the Mississippi and Missouri statehouses, the Maryland State House.

state of the art. It means the current level of sophistication. Do not use as a synonym for high tech or fancy.

State of the Union message, State of the Union address

states. When the name of a state appears as part of a complete mailing address and in college-book tables, use the Postal Service abbreviation. Otherwise, use the traditional abbreviation. (In a very tight spot on a map or chart, *Cal., Col., Ia., Ida., Me.,* and *Tex.* may be used.)

STATE NAME	ABBREVIATION IN ADDRESSES	TRADITIONAL ABBREVIATION	NAME OF RESIDENT(S)
Alabama	AL	Ala.	Alabamian(s)
Alaska	AK	none	Alaskan(s)
Arizona	AZ	Ariz.	Arizonan(s)
Arkansas	AR	Ark.	Arkansan(s)
California	CA	Calif.	Californian(s)
Colorado	CO	Colo.	Coloradan(s)
Connecticut	CT	Conn.	Connecticuter(s)
Delaware	DE	Del.	Delawarean(s)
District of Columbia	DC	D.C.	District of Columbia resident(s), District resident(s), D.C. resident(s) Washingtonian(s)
Florida	FL	Fla.	Floridian(s)
Georgia	GA	Ga.	Georgian(s)
Hawaii	HI	none	Hawaiian(s)
Idaho	ID	none	Idahoan(s)
Illinois	IL	Ill.	Illinoisan(s)
Indiana	IN	Ind.	Indianan(s)
Iowa	IA	none	Iowan(s)
Kansas	KS	Kan.	Kansan(s)
Kentucky	KY	Ky.	Kentuckian(s)
Louisiana	LA	La.	Louisianian(s)
Maine	ME	none	Mainer(s)
Maryland	MD	Md.	Marylander(s)
Massachusetts	MA	Mass.	Massachusetts resident(s), Bay Stater(s), Massachusettsan(s)
Michigan	MI	Mich.	Michigander(s) Michiganian(s)
Minnesota	MN	Minn.	Minnesotan(s)
Mississippi	MS	Miss.	Mississippian(s)
Missouri	MO	Mo.	Missourian(s)
Montana	MT	Mont.	Montanan(s)
Nebraska	NE	Neb.	Nebraskan(s)
Nevada	NV	Nev.	Nevadan(s)
New Hampshire	NH	N.H.	New Hampshirite(s)
New Jersey	NJ	N.J.	New Jerseyite(s)
New Mexico	NM	N.M.	New Mexican(s)
New York	NY	N.Y.	New Yorker(s)
North Carolina	NC	N.C.	North Carolinian(s)
North Dakota	ND	N.D.	North Dakotan(s)
Ohio	OH	none	Ohioan(s)

STATE NAME	ABBREVIATION IN ADDRESSES	TRADITIONAL ABBREVIATION	NAME OF RESIDENT(S)
Oklahoma	OK	Okla.	Oklahoman(s)
Oregon	OR	Ore.	Oregonian(s)
Pennsylvania	PA	Pa.	Pennsylvanian(s)
Rhode Island	RI	R.I.	Rhode Islander(s)
South Carolina	SC	S.C.	South Carolinian(s)
South Dakota	SD	S.D.	South Dakotan(s)
Tennessee	TN	Tenn.	Tennessean(s)
Texas	TX	none	Texan(s)
Utah	UT	none	Utahn(s)
Vermont	VT	Vt.	Vermonter(s)
Virginia	VA	Va.	Virginian(s)
Washington	WA	Wash.	Washingtonian(s)
West Virginia	WV	W.Va.	West Virginian(s)
Wisconsin	WI	Wis.	Wisconsinite(s)
Wyoming	WY	Wyo.	Wyomingite(s)

(Kentucky, Massachusetts, Pennsylvania, and Virginia are formally commonwealths but should be called states in all but legal references.) See POLITICAL REGIONS.

States, the. Capitalize when referring to the United States as a country: on return to the States, but the states of the nation.

staunch/stanch. Staunch means steadfast or loyal; stanch means to stop the flow.

Stealth. Unofficial name for the B-2A bomber and the F-117A fighter.

steelmaker

St.-John's-wort

stockholder, but common-stock holder

stocks and bonds. Use figures to indicate types of stocks and bonds: sale of $2^1/_2$s increased.

storm. Capitalize when personified: Tropical Storm Tessie (the tropical storm), Hurricane Hank. Use it, not *she* or *he*.

Strategic Arms Limitation Treaty, but strategic arms treaty, strategic arms limitation talks. SALT is acceptable as a second reference to both the treaty and the talks. SALT II.

Street. Spell out and capitalize when part of an address. See ADDRESSES.

strewn (past participle of strew)

stubs. See CHARTS AND TABLES.

styles in the arts. See CULTURAL DESIGNATIONS.

sub( ). Combines solid except before a capital letter (sub-Saharan) or in Latin phrases, such as sub judice.

subcommittee. Capitalize in names of legislative groups: the Senate Consumer and Regulatory Affairs Subcommittee (the Senate Consumer Affairs Subcommittee). Lowercase alone and when not the actual name: the subcommittee, a Senate Banking subcommittee. See COMMITTEE.

subheads. Do not place sideheads earlier than the second paragraph of a story or directly before the kicker in a story.

subject-verb agreement. AND. When *and* joins more than one subject, the verb is almost always plural, even when the subjects are separated by commas or dashes: Pedro, and his friend Whitney, were the first to arrive. An exception is when multiple subjects represent a single idea: Peanut butter and jelly is a favorite among the soccer players.

AS WELL AS, WITH, IN ADDITION TO, INCLUDING, ETC. When expressions like these join multiple subjects, the verb takes the number of the principal subject: Pedro, as well as Whitney, was the first to arrive.

such as. See LIKE, AS.

suffixes. See HYPHEN.

suffragette/suffragist. Suffragette may be used for references to certain militant feminists of the early 20th century, particularly in Britain, but it was used primarily in the United States as a label of disparagement by opponents of woman's suffrage, so, for general purposes, use suffragist, which is the term that feminists like Susan B. Anthony applied to themselves.

summit conference. the Bush-Qadhafi summit conference (the summit).

sun. Lowercase except when personified: the sun, a sun, suns, "Sisters of the Sun are gonna get down to the sea somehow." See **HEAVENLY BODIES.**

Sun Belt

super( ). Combines solid except before a capitalization, a double word, or a doubled *r:* superconducting supercollider, supercarrier, **but** super aircraft carrier, super giant slalom (super G), super-reactor, We had a super time.

Super Bowl, Super Bowl XXIV, the bowl

superintendent. Capitalize before a name as a title; lowercase otherwise. Abbreviate, supt., only in charts, maps, and tables.

Super Tuesday. Capitalize such references to special days.

Supreme Court. the U.S. Supreme Court (the Supreme Court, the court), the Arkansas Supreme Court (the state Supreme Court, the Supreme Court), a state's supreme court (**descriptive**). Caution: *Supreme Court* does not always refer to a jurisdiction's highest court. The New York Supreme Court, for example, is a trial court; the highest court in New York is the Court of Appeals.

surgeon general. Capitalize before a name; lowercase otherwise: Surgeon General Amy Brenneman (the surgeon general). **Do not abbreviate.**

SUV. Acceptable for sport utility vehicle when the meaning is clear.

symposium(s). Capitalize in an official name; lowercase otherwise: the Itinerant Symposium on the Granites of Northeast, the symposium, the Hamburg symposium on protection of seacoasts against pollution.

Synagogue. Capitalize in names of congregations; lowercase otherwise: Beth Israel Synagogue (the synagogue). See **JEWISH CONGREGATIONS.**

table. Capitalize with a number or a letter: Table 2, Table B.

tables. See CHARTS AND TABLES.

take-home (noun and adjective): How much is your take-home? I could use more take-home pay.

Talmud

tanks. Write U.S. tank designations solid; hyphenate Russian designations. Follow the designations used in *Jane's Armour:* M1, M2, M60A3 (U.S.), T-34, T-54 (Russian), AMX-30 (French).

(-)tax (adjective). income-tax rise, property-tax payment.

taxpayer, but income-tax payer

teachers college

telephone numbers. (800) 555-1212, Ext. 501. When the number is already in parentheses, or where space is tight in a chart or table, drop the parentheses around the area code and add a hyphen: Phone home (215-682-1212) today. In general, avoid using letters in place of numbers.

television. Put the names of series in italics: *I Love Lucy.* Make the names of episodes roman with quotes: "Ricky Foils Show Scheme." The names of characters are roman, no quotes: Lucy Ricardo.

television rating symbols.
TV-Y suitable for children of all ages
TV-Y7 suitable for children 7 and older
TV-G suitable for all audiences
TV-PG parental guidance suggested
TV-14 may be inappropriate for children under 14
TV-MA designed to be viewed by adults and therefore may be unsuitable for children under 17

temperature. Use figures to indicate number of degrees. Except in tabular matter or series, spell out *degrees* and the designation of the scale being used. In tables or series, abbreviations or the degree symbol may be used: 7 degrees below zero Fahrenheit (abbreviation: –7°F); It was 10 below; a 15-degree difference; between 5 and 6 degrees Celsius (abbreviation: 5° to 6°C). See METRIC SYSTEM.

temple. Capitalize in names of congregations; lowercase alone: Beth El Temple, the temple. See JEWISH CONGREGATIONS.

Tennessean

Tennessee (Tenn., TN in addresses)

tenses. See HEDGING.

terrorism, terrorist. Limit the use of these words to politically motivated violent acts that are directed against noncombatants without regard for innocent lives. In a military context, *guerrilla* is a less politically loaded word to describe unconventional warfare. Write that people who admit such acts take responsibility for them, not that they *take credit for* them.

Texan

Texas (TX in addresses. Otherwise abbreviate, Tex., only in a tight spot on charts, maps, or tables.)

that, which. Descriptive (nonrestrictive) clauses are set off by commas and take a *which:* The Band, which performed in Cambridge, had five members. Defining (restrictive) clauses are not set off by commas and usually take a *that:* The band that played yesterday broke up today.

that/who. Refer to animals as *that* and *which,* unless they are named: She chased the deer, which was fast; He rode Stewball, who was slow.

the. See BOOK TITLES, COMPANY NAMES, MAGAZINES, and NEWSPAPERS.

theater, but follow a particular theater's spelling in a name: Kreeger Theater, Ford's Theatre, the theater.

then. then President Bartlett, the then married couple.

thin space is used to regularize spacing between certain elements and to keep intact elements that the computer would otherwise allow to break erroneously from one line to the next. For example, a thin space is used with subquotation marks and quotation marks ("She said, 'Don't Go.' "), with ellipses ("They are married . . . with children"), and between initials (T. G. Shepherd). Create by hitting ctrl/shift/space bar.

third. Use roman numerals after a name: Robert Stein III.

Third World

this week. It refers to the week preceding the cover date. So a person whose birthday falls during the week that begins with the cover date, for example, would be identified with the younger age. Each week begins on Monday and ends on Sunday.

thoroughbred

time. Use figures for clock time (3 p.m., 5:30 a.m., 6 o'clock) and for hours, minutes, seconds, days, weeks, months, and years greater than nine. Spell out for nine and less, except in reference to the age of an animate object (She was 9 years old. She lived there nine years. She lived there 13 weeks), when a fraction is connected to a whole number ($2^1/_2$ hours), or in combination with figures above nine (The nurse spoke for 2 days and 13 hours). Avoid such redundancies as *10 o'clock p.m.* and *12 noon.* Midnight is the end of a day, not the beginning. Don't use *12 a.m.* or *12 p.m.* Write noon or midnight.

time and a half. He was paid time and a half. She received time-and-a-half pay.

time elements. See HEDGING and THIS WEEK.

times greater, times smaller. See GREATER THAN, AS GREAT AS.

time zones. Capitalize the full name and abbreviate or spell out as appropriate: Eastern Standard Time (EST), Eastern Daylight Time (EDT), Pacific Standard Time, Greenwich Mean Time, but the Eastern time zone, Eastern time, daylight-saving time. At 6:25 a.m. CST he left the hospital and drove home.

titles of nobility. See NOBILITY and TITLES OF PERSONS.

titles of persons. Capitalize titles when used as such before names; lowercase them when they follow the name, when they are used in apposition before a name, when they are standing alone, and when qualifying words make them more descriptive than titular:

EXECUTIVE. President Watson (the president); running for president; former President Wenta (the former president); Italian President Ernesto Troia, **but** Italy's president, Silvio Dante; Presidents Watson and Dante (the presidents); Premier Li Soon (Premier Soon, the premier); Gov. Katharine Vassar (Governor Vassar, the governor).

ADMINISTRATIVE. Secretary of State Colin Powell (the secretary of state, the secretary), Secretaries of State Powell and Albright, Deputy Secretary of State Earl Rosenberg (the deputy secretary of state), Attorney General Frederick Vondy (the attorney general), Secretary of the Navy John Zappardino (the secretary of the Navy, the secretary), Foreign Minister Qian Qichen (the foreign minister), Director of Central Intelligence Vincent Long (the director), Press Secretary Paul Schurick (the press secretary), Chairman Reed Hundt of the Federal Communications Commission (FCC Chairman Hundt, the FCC chairman).

LEGISLATIVE. Sen. Paul McAdams (Senator McAdams, the senator); Rep. Marianne Sherwood (Representative Sherwood, the representative); Senate Majority Leader Carolyn Wood (Majority Leader Carolyn Wood, the majority leader); Holmes Elliott, president pro tem of the Senate; Speaker of the House Lindsey Warren (House Speaker Lindsey Warren, the speaker).

JUDICIAL. Chief Justice Emmylou Basham (the chief justice), Associate Justice Royd Luedde (Justice Royd Luedde, Justice Luedde, the associate justice, the justice), Chief Judge Roland Kelley (Judge Kelley, the chief judge, the judge).

RELIGIOUS. Pope John Paul II (Pope John Paul, the pope), the Rev. Betsy Haller.

POLITICAL. Democratic National Chairman Fred Manjone (Fred Manjone, the Democratic national chairman, the chairman).

ROYALTY. Princess Tina of Belgium (Princess Tina, the princess).

NOBILITY. Treat titles like sir, dame, lord, and lady as you would honorifics, i.e., don't use them unless they are in direct quotations or are needed for clarity. Capitalize only when they are used as a title before a name.

BUSINESS. Chief Executive Officer Barney Tassler (the chief executive officer, the chief executive), Managing Editor Jesse Leedy (the managing editor, editor Leedy).

OCCUPATIONAL DESCRIPTIONS are lowercase: fashion designer Lauren Tullier, sports editor Glen Edgerton, astronaut Tom Hanks, park ranger Marsha Selko, parts department manager George Martinez, first baseman Lou Gehrig, cellist Gregor Piatigorsky. When you encounter difficulty drawing the line between a title and an occupational description, a safe bet is to lowercase the description and put it after the name or set it off in apposition before the name with commas: the paper's sports editor, Glen Edgerton, was honored. When qualifying words make a title more like a description than a title, the title may be spelled out and lowercased: career ambassador Logan Winter; European-history professor Jill Farace; defeated Florida governor Bob Martinez; retired majority leader Sarah Collins, but be consistent within an editorial package. Don't use double titles, such as *the Rev. Dr. Willy Wirtz.* See MILITARY TITLES, NOBILITY, YOUR HONOR, and individual listings (CHAIR, POPE, QUEEN, SENATOR, etc.).

titles of works. Capitalize principal words and prepositions and conjunctions of more than three letters. For readability, make all-cap and all-lowercase titles caps and lowercase unless they are acronyms or initialisms. Use the following typographical conventions regardless of the medium (paper, film, video, floppy disk, CD-ROM, etc.) in which the work appears.

ITALICS, NO QUOTES	ROMAN, QUOTES	ROMAN, NO QUOTES
almanacs	articles	books of the Bible
ballets	booklets	computer operating
books	chapters	systems
collections of poetry	dissertations	computer programs,
comic books	episodes of radio and	like for word
comic strips	television programs	processing and
dictionaries	essays	spreadsheets
encyclopedias	exhibitions	games
law reviews	headlines	historical documents,
long musical compositions	lectures	like the Declaration
with distinctive names	monographs	of Independence,
long poems published	pamphlets	the Magna Carta,
separately	reports	and the Gettysburg
magazines	short poems	Address
medical journals	short stories	Internet browsers

ITALICS, NO QUOTES	ROMAN, QUOTES	ROMAN, NO QUOTES
movies	songs	musical compositions
newsletters	speeches	named by number
newspapers	theses	or key
operas		names of Web sites
oratorios		online services
paintings		sacred religious books,
photographs		like the Bible, the
plays		Koran, the Torah,
radio and television series		and the Bhagavad
record albums		Gita
sculpture		
textbooks		
uniform resource locators		
(URLs)		

See BOOK TITLES, COMPUTER PROGRAMS, HEADLINES, MAGAZINES, MUSICAL COMPOSITIONS, and NEWSPAPERS.

ton. 2,000 pounds (short ton). Abbreviation, t, acceptable in charts and tables when the meaning is clear. Long ton (2,240 pounds) is used in Britain. A metric ton is 1,000 kilograms (about 2,200 pounds).

touchpad

touch-screen

townhouse/town house. A townhouse is a dwelling, usually of two or three stories, in a planned cluster of contiguous buildings in either the city or the suburbs; a town house is a city residence, usually so designated because the owner also has a place in the country.

toxin refers only to naturally produced substances. Do not use as a synonym for all toxic substances.

track and field (noun and adjective)

trackball

trademarks. A word or symbol used by a company to identify its goods or services, a trademark is legally protected from use by the owner's competitors and generally should not be lowercased or used in such a way that it seems to be a common noun, adjective, or verb. Use a generic equivalent rather than a trademark unless a point is being made about a particular trademarked article or the trademark is deemed helpful in setting a scene. Thus for identity's sake we might write about a strike at a plant where Coca-Cola is bottled, but if we feel a brand reference is helpful when we write about "a labor dispute over operation of the Coke machine," we should (for accuracy's sake) be absolutely certain it is a Coke machine, and if we are not sure, we should describe it generically, as, for example, a "soft-drink machine" or a "vending machine." If trademarks are not guarded from use in senses that seem generic, they may officially lose protection of the law and can be employed thereafter by all companies. When this happens, there is no longer any restriction on writers. Former trademarks that have passed into the public domain include: aspirin, cellophane, cornflakes, cube steak, dry ice, escalator, kerosene, lanolin, linoleum, milk of magnesia, mimeograph, nylon, raisin bran, shredded wheat, thermos, touch-tone, trampoline, zipper. As a good corporate citizen, *U.S. News,* which protects trademarks of its own, should strive to avoid misuse of other companies' trademarks. At the same time, we must be attuned to language evolution that turns hitherto-protected words into colorful and useful generic expressions. When you refer to a specific trademarked product, capitalize it: Braise the trout in a Teflon skillet. They sold Band-Aids at the checkout counter. When use of a brand name does not help the story or you are unsure of the brand, use a generic equivalent: Braise the trout in a skillet with a nonstick coating. They sold adhesive bandages at the checkout counter. Use a brand name generically only when such use is sanctioned by the dictionary: She dubbed Reagan "the teflon president." The treasurer said the bill amounted to "nothing more than a band-aid solution to the problem." Sources of information about trademarks, including new marks and others not listed in this entry:

1. *Standard Directory of Advertisers*
2. Checklist of the International Trademark Association. Telephone inquiries: (212) 768-9886, daily 2 p.m. to 5 p.m. Web list: *www.inta.org.*
3. For drugs, *Physicians' Desk Reference*

TRADEMARK	GENERIC
A.1.	sauce
Acrilan	acrylic fiber
Advil	ibuprofen pain reliever
Airfoam	sponge and cellular rubber
Anchor Fence	chain-link fence
AstroTurf	artificial turf
Aureomycin	antibiotic
Avril	rayon
Baggies	plastic bags
Band-Aid	adhesive bandage
Brillo	soap pad
Celanese	yarns, fabrics

TRADEMARK	GENERIC
Chex	cereal
Chiclets	chewing gum
Chloromycetin	antibiotic
Clorox	bleach
Coca-Cola, Coke	soft drink, cola drink
Congoleum	floor coverings
Contac	antihistamine, decongestant
Cream of Wheat	cereal
Crescent	adjustable wrench
Crisco	shortening
Cyclone	chain-link fence
Dacron	polyester fiber
Day-Glo	fluorescent paints, etc.
Day-Timer	scheduler, schedule book
Disposall	food-waste disposers
Dramamine	travel-sickness medicine
Dynel	modacrylic fiber
Electrolux	vacuum cleaner
Eveready	batteries
Fiberglas	fiberglass, glass fibers
Fig Newtons	fruited cakes
Flit	insecticide
Formica	laminated plastic
Fortrel	polyester yarn
Frigidaire	refrigerator, appliances
Frisbee	plastic flying disk
Fritos	corn chips
Fudgsicle	ice cream on a stick
Gatorade	sports drink
Go Kart	go-cart
Gripper	snap fasteners
Hamburger Helper	packaged dinner mixes
Hawaiian Punch	fruit beverage
Jell-O	gelatin dessert
Jet Ski	personal watercraft
Jockey	underwear
Jonny Mop	toilet bowl cleaner
Kleenex	tissues
Kodachrome	film
Kodacolor	film
Kodak	film and cameras
Kodel	polyester
Kool-Aid	soft-drink mix
Kotex	sanitary napkins, belts, tampons
Levi's	jeans and sportswear
Liederkranz	cheese

T

TRADEMARK	GENERIC
Linotype	typesetting machine
Lucite	acrylic resin
Lycra	spandex fiber
Lysol	disinfectant
Mace	liquid tear-gas formulation
Masonite	hardboard products
Maypo	cereal
Mazola	margarine and corn oil
Mercurochrome	antiseptic
Miltown	tranquilizer
Minute	rice
Mixmaster	food mixer
Muzak	music programs
Naugahyde	vinyl-coated fabrics
Neolite	composition soles and heels
Nescafé	instant coffee
Novocain	novocaine, anesthetic
Nutrament	food supplement
Orlon	acrylic fiber
Ouija	"talking board" sets
Oysterettes	crackers
Pablum	pabulum, baby cereal
Parcheesi	board game
Pepsi-Cola, Pepsi	soft drink, cola drink
Photostat	photographic copy
Ping-Pong	table tennis equipment
Playtex	girdles and bras
Plexiglas	acrylic plastic, plexiglass
Polaroid	photographic equipment or polarizing sunglasses
Popsicle	frozen confection
Post Toasties	cereal
Prestone	antifreeze
Pyrex	heat-resistant glassware
Q-Tips	cotton swabs
Realtor	real-estate broker, agent, specialist
Ritz	crackers
Rollerblade	in-line skates
Rotisserie League	fantasy baseball, football, etc.
Sanforized	preshrunk fabric
Scotch	cellophane tape
Scrabble	word game
7 Up	soft drink
Sheetrock	gypsum wallboard
Styrofoam	plastic foam
Sucrets	medicated lozenges

T

TRADEMARK	GENERIC
Sunbeam	appliances
Sunkist	fruit and juices
Tabasco	sauce
Technicolor	motion-picture color process
Teflon	nonstick coating
Teletype	communications equipment
Terramycin	antibiotic
Thiokol	liquid polymers
Thorazine	tranquilizer
Tinkertoy	construction toy
Toastmaster	electric appliances
Tylenol	acetaminophen pain reliever
Unicap	vitamins
Valium	tranquilizer
Vaseline	petroleum jelly, lip balm
Velcro	hook-and-loop fastener, touch fastener
Walkman	personal stereo(s)
Xerox	xerographic copiers
Zepel	fabric water repellent
Zerex	antifreeze
ZipNut	push-on nut

See ADRENALINE AND JEEP.

trans( ). Combines solid except before capitalization: transmundane, trans-Atlantic.

transsexual/transvestite. A transsexual is a person whose primary sexual identification is with the opposite sex, often using surgery and/or drugs to effect a sex change; a transvestite, also called a cross-dresser, is a person who wears clothing usually identified with the opposite sex.

treasury. Capitalize in the name of the cabinet department (Department of the Treasury, Treasury Department), in titles when they precede a person's name (Secretary of the Treasury Helen Myers, Treasury Secretary Helen Myers), and when standing alone and when necessary for clarity: Treasury was the target of severe layoffs. (But avoid overusing the latter construction, which sounds jargonistic.) Lowercase other references: Helen Myers, the treasury secretary; treasury bill, treasuries, but T-bill, T-bills.

treaty. Capitalize as part of an official name; lowercase alone: Treaty of Versailles (Versailles Treaty, the treaty). See the electronic NAMES list.

trillion. See MILLION.

tropical storm. Tropical Storm Wendy (the tropical storm); **use it, not** *she* or *he.*

turned. Do not hyphenate such constructions as editor turned plumber.

twin-engine (adjective)

two-by-four (noun and adjective)

(-)type. Hyphenate when used as an adjective meaning "of that sort": a Western-type saddle, **but** He was a Hollywood type.

typhoid, typhus. Typhoid (fever) is a salmonella-caused disease; typhus is caused by rickettsia bacteria and is transmitted by bites from fleas or lice.

up-to-dateness

ultra( ). Combines solid except before a capital letter or an *a.*

un( ). Combines solid except before a capital letter.

U.N. Acceptable after first reference to United Nations. See UNITED NATIONS.

under( ). Generally combines solid except before capitalization, but under secretary.

Underground Railroad. Capitalize references to the system used to move American slaves to freedom: Harriet Tubman was the Underground Railroad's primary conductor; the railroad.

under secretary. Capitalize as a title before a name; lowercase otherwise: Under Secretary of State Carol Stroll (the under secretary of state, the under secretary).

understrength

union. Capitalize when it refers to the Northern states during the Civil War: the states of the Union.

union names. Capitalize union when it is part of a labor union name or a paraphrase thereof; lowercase otherwise: Teamsters Union, United Automobile, Aerospace, and Agricultural Implement Workers of America (United Auto Workers Union, United Auto Workers, the auto union, the union). Follow union style on use of apostrophes: International Ladies' Garment Workers Union, Directors Guild of America. Use *and,* not an ampersand, in union names.

United Kingdom is Britain (England, Scotland, and Wales) and Northern Ireland. The British Isles consist of Britain, Ireland, and adjacent islands, including the Isle of Man and the Channel Islands.

United Methodist Church. Some nonordained persons serve in special capacities as deacons. They may be described as such but are not officially referred to by a title or an honorific like *the Rev.* When a layperson "supplies" a church (serves it as pastor), it is a customary courtesy to put *the Rev.* before the person's name. Ordained persons first become deacons, then elders. All ordained persons are referred to as *the Rev.* Either a deacon or an elder may be a pastor; to hold a position higher than pastor, one must be an elder. All titles are used for men and women alike. Women as well as men can be deacons, pastors, and bishops. Eighth Street United Methodist Church (the church); the Rev. Harwood Johnson, pastor of Eighth Street United Methodist Church (the pastor, Johnson); Bishop Harwood Johnson of the Kentucky Conference (Bishop Johnson, the bishop, Johnson).

United Nations (U.N.). United Nations Charter (the charter), Security Council (the council), General Assembly (the Assembly), Secretary General Robert Cooke (the secretary general, the secretariat).

United States (U.S., U.S.A.). the States (referring to the nation), the states (referring to the individual states). Abbreviations are acceptable only when used as an adjective and in quotes, headlines, charts, maps, and tables. The possessive is United States'. See WE.

university. Capitalize in a name; lowercase alone: Brigham Young University (the university). See COLLEGES AND UNIVERSITIES.

Untouchable(s). Capitalize references to members of the caste.

upper. See CENTRAL.

up-to-dateness. The problem is not only that a court case may have been dismissed or appealed. Bills in a legislature may have been passed or defeated, lost people may have been found, feuding politicians may have made up, local prices may have risen, building projects may have been abandoned. Even if our story was correct when written yesterday, something may have happened since. When feasible, both the writer and the editors should look out for things that could change and, where possible, update them before publication.

URL(s). Acceptable for uniform (or universal) resource locator(s) when clear. URLs are usually set italic: *www.usnews.com.* When a URL breaks over a line, drop the line-break hyphen:

Carla said the best place to find
articulated worms is *www.worms
rus.com.*

us. See WE.

USA. Acceptable, when clear, for references to the United States Army.

U.S.A. See UNITED STATES.

USAF. Acceptable, when clear, for references to the United States Air Force.

U.S. attorney. Capitalize before a name; lowercase otherwise. Keep the *U.S.* after first reference or use another word, like *prosecutor,* to avoid confusion.

USMC. Acceptable, when clear, for references to the United States Marine Corps.

USN. Acceptable, when clear, for United States Navy, U.S. Navy. USNR: United States Naval Reserve, U.S. Naval Reserve.

USN&WR. Abbreviation used in credits.

U.S. News is for general use of the name. Put a space between *U.S.* and *News.* For the formal name, *U.S.News & World Report,* use no space between *U.S.* and *News.*

USS (United States Ship)

Utah (UT in addresses; do not abbreviate otherwise)

Utahan is an adjective meaning of or from Utah. Utahn is a noun meaning a resident of Utah.

utopia, utopian. Lowercase except in references to the place in Thomas More's book.

When quoting a poem remember
the rule / Run lines together
and use a virgule.

verse

v. Use, italicized, for versus in legal citations: *Jones v. NLRB.* See VS.

VA. Acceptable on second reference to the Department of Veterans Affairs as well as to its predecessor, the Veterans' Administration.

Valley. Capitalize when part of a real or fanciful name; lowercase otherwise: Red River Valley, Silicon Valley, Happy Valley (the valley).

van. See PARTICLES.

V-chip

VCR. Acceptable for videocassette recorder.

V-E Day, V-J Day

veep

venetian. venetian red, venetian blinds, but Venetian glass (made in or near Venice).

verbal. See ORAL/VERBAL.

verdict/judgment/settlement. A verdict is rendered by a judge or a jury, and it can result in a judgment, which is "awarded" by the court. A settlement, which is "reached" or "agreed to," is a voluntary agreement by both sides in a civil trial.

Vermont (Vt., VT in addresses)

Vermonter

verse. Run lines together, separated by thin spaces on both sides of a virgule: He thought it happier to be dead, / To die for beauty, than live for bread.

versus. Use *v.* for court citations; otherwise, use vs. or versus.

Very Rev. See EPISCOPAL CHURCH and ROMAN CATHOLIC CHURCH.

Veterans Day

vice. vice admiral, vice chairman, vice president, vice presidency, vice presidential, vice regent, viceroy, vice squad.

vice president. Capitalize before a name; lowercase otherwise: Vice President Jon Baron (the vice president). First names of American vice presidents need not be used on first reference with the title unless confusion would otherwise result.

vice/vise. Vice is evil or wicked conduct; a vise is a tool.

victim. Keep in mind that some people consider the word sensational in such uses as a polio victim or an AIDS victim. People with such conditions generally do not like language that suggests their lives are tragic or to be pitied. Preferred are such constructions as a person with polio. *Victim* is considered offensive because most such people do not see themselves as victims, nor do they want to be seen as victims. Likewise, the use of *patient* for a person who is not hospitalized or undergoing treatment is considered offensive because it suggests someone to be pitied, when a person with cerebral palsy or a similar condition may in fact be in otherwise excellent health and live a long life. See DISABLED and HANDICAP.

video. video arcade, video camera, video display terminal, video game, video programs, videotape recording, videocassette, videocassette recorder, videoconferencing, videodisk.

video games. Make titles roman, no quotes: Super Mario.

Vietnam Veterans Memorial. See WALL, THE.

Viking

Virginia (Va., VA in addresses)

Virginian

Virgin Islands (V.I., VI in addresses). Inhabitants are residents of the Virgin Islands.

visitor center. Follow a specific center's spelling and capitalization for formal names, but make generic references singular and lowercase: the Lake Hope Visitors' Center, the visitor center.

vitamin. vitamin A, vitamin B12.

voice. See ACTIVE VOICE.

von. See PARTICLES.

vote getter

vote tabulations. Use figures: The clean-air bill was approved 347 to 29. A 347-to-29 margin or, where space is at a premium, as in headlines and captions, a 347-29 margin.

vs. Acceptable abbreviation for *versus,* except in legal citations, where it is *v.* Both letters are lowercase, except in the event vs. begins a sentence or a headline, in which case it is Vs. See V.

vulgarity. See OBSCENITY, PROFANITY, VULGARITY.

VW. Acceptable for Volkswagen on second reference.

V

wall, the. When used as a nickname for a structure whose name does not include the word *wall,* such as the Vietnam Veterans Memorial, put the first such reference in quotation marks (It was Ken's first visit to "the wall"). But when used alone to refer to a structure with *wall* in its name, write it lowercase, without quotation marks: Ellen clutched a piece of the Berlin Wall (the wall).

wangle/wrangle. Wangle means to bring about by persuasion or trickery; wrangle means to quarrel angrily and noisily, or to herd.

wannabe(s). Acceptable as a noun when context makes the meaning clear. For adjectival use, *would-be* is better.

war. Capitalize in names of past, current, and future wars; lowercase alone: Korean War (the war), Spanish Civil War, Vietnam War, World War I, First World War, World War II, Second World War, World War III, the next world war, a world war, the world wars, Gulf War, Cold War, Yom Kippur War, the Civil War (U.S.), but the civil war in Lebanon, Lebanese civil war. See the electronic NAMES list.

War Between the States. Used as a reference to the U.S. Civil War by those sympathetic to the Confederacy.

ward. Capitalize in a name; lowercase alone: Fourth Ward, 16th Ward (the ward).

war front

war maker

warrant officer. See MILITARY TITLES.

Washington (Wash., WA in addresses). When there is the possibility of confusion with Washington, D.C., write Washington State or the state of Washington.

Washington, D.C. (do not abbreviate *Washington*). D.C. is not necessary as long as there is no possibility of confusion with Washington State.

Washingtonian. A resident of the state of Washington or of the District of Columbia.

waste water

( )watcher. China watcher, China watching, but bird-watcher and bird-watching.

we. In headlines, *we* could variously mean corporate *U.S. News*, its owner, its editors, its reporters, its readers, "right-minded" people, human beings, Americans, earthlings, scientists, or subgroups thereof. So in general, avoid using first-person singular and plural. Except in columns and editorials, do not use *we, us, our,* and *ours* when referring to the United States or the American people.

weapons. *Jane's Weapon Systems* is a helpful guide, but note some cases in which *U.S. News* style varies from *Jane's.* See FIREARMS.

( )wear. Combinations are usually solid: neckwear, sportswear, outdoorwear, menswear.

weather phenomena. Capitalize when personified: Hurricane Tessie (the hurricane), Tropical Storm Henry (the tropical storm). Use it, not *he* or *she.*

Web. Acceptable when clear on references to the World Wide Web: the Web, Web site. Lowercase one-word combinations: webmaster, webzine, webhead.

The names of Web sites are generally roman: Girl Tech. Web addresses should generally be italicized *(http://www.girltech.com)* or set in some other distinctive type. Follow a Web site's spelling and capitalization (eBay, iBUY), but capitalize the first letter when the name begins a sentence (EBay delayed its announcement). Online periodicals are italicized (It appeared in the online magazine *Slate*). See COMPANY NAMES.

week. Capitalize in the name of a specially designated period: Holy Week, National Safety Week.

week, this. "This week" refers to the week preceding the cover date. So a person whose birthday falls during the week that begins with the cover date, for example, would be identified with the younger age. Each week begins on Monday and ends on Sunday.

weeklong

weightlifting, weightlifter

weights and measures. Use figures: 13 inches; 6 pounds; 9 miles; 120 volts; she was 5 feet, 2 inches tall; a 5-foot, 2-inch woman.

ABBREVIATIONS. Btu, mpg, mph and rpm may be used on all references in an article if the meaning is clear. Hp and psi may be used on second reference in an article. The other abbreviations should be used only in charts, maps, and tables. Singular abbreviations are both singular and plural.

barrel(s)	bbl.	miles per hour	mph
British thermal unit(s)	Btu	minute(s)	min.
bushel(s)	bu.	ounce(s)	oz.
calorie(s)	cal.	pound(s)	lb.
dollar(s)	$	pounds per square inch	psi
foot (feet)	ft.	quarter	qtr., q.
gallon(s)	gal.	revolutions per minute	rpm
horsepower	hp	second(s)	sec.
hour(s)	hr.	ton(s)	t.
inch(es)	in.	yard(s)	yd.
mile(s)	mi.	year(s)	yr.
miles per gallon	mpg		

See METRIC SYSTEM, NUMBERS, and TIME.

well(-). When combining with an adjective before a noun, hyphenate: well-prepared student, well-versed writer, well-known actor, but very well known actor. When the combination is used after the noun, drop the hyphen unless the result would be confusing: He was well preserved. Her back was well massaged. The raise was well deserved.

welsh. Use only in quotations and then only when essential to a story. Acceptable alternatives include cheat, swindle, renege, and evade.

west, western. Capitalize in a name and when designating a region; lowercase when merely giving a direction: driving out West (but driving west), the Old West, West Coast, Western world, Western Europe, Western Hemisphere, Western states, Western movie (a Western), Westerner, West Africa, West End (of London), but westbound, western pine, western omelet, country and western music, westernize. See COMPASS DIRECTIONS.

Western allies, but the Allies and Allied powers in World War II. See ALLIES, ALLIED.

West Virginia (W.Va., WV in addresses)

West Virginian

wheelchairbound. Disabled people find terms such as this and "confined to a wheelchair" offensive, believing that they generally exaggerate one's inability. Except for some cases of quadriplegia, people can get in and out of wheelchairs, usually by themselves. We would not write "eyeglassbound." Preferred terminology includes: uses a wheelchair, a wheelchair user.

which. See THAT, WHICH.

whip. Capitalize as a title before a name; lowercase otherwise.

whiskey(s)/whisky (whiskies). Use whisky for Scotch whisky and Canadian whisky. Use whiskey for all other references: bourbon whiskey, rye whiskey, whiskey sour.

white paper. Lowercase unless part of a name.

who/whom. Perhaps *whom* will someday bite the dust, but until it does, use it properly: Whom do you trust? (*whom* is the object of the verb *trust*). Who is going to the dance? (*who* is the subject). Who shall I say called? (*who* is the subject). The friends whom Peter framed were set free (*whom* is the object of *framed*). The friends who Manny said were present signed up (*who* is the subject, hidden from its verb, *were,* by *Manny said*). Whoever said we should work here is brilliant (*Whoever* is the subject of *is*).

( )wide. Combines solid: citywide, companywide, countrywide, industrywide, nationwide, plantwide, statewide, worldwide.

wife, husband. Use commas: Bob brought his wife, Melissa, home (unless he has more than one wife).

windfall-profits tax

Wisconsin (Wis., WI in addresses)

Wisconsinite

( )wise. When the word denotes a way or manner, it usually combines solid: lengthwise. Meaning sage, it usually is hyphenated: penny-wise.

woman/female. In general, when a noun is called for in referring to a woman, use *woman,* and when an adjective is called for, use *female.*

( ) word. When you use such expressions as the "L" word, put the letter in quotation marks.

words as words. Italicize: He inserted an *and* into the record.

workday/workaday/work-day. A workday is a day on which work is done; workaday means everyday or commonplace; a work-day is a measure of the amount of work a person does in one day.

( )worker. Make combinations not in the dictionary two words: autoworker, factory worker, farm-implement worker, farmworker, ironworker, metalworker, mineworker, office worker, steelworker.

workers' compensation. Use plural even if only one person is involved: She filed for workers' compensation, a workers' compensation suit.

workforce

work-hour. A measure of the amount of work a person does in one hour.

workplace

works of art. Use italics: Michelangelo's *Madonna of the Stairs*. See TI-TLES OF WORKS.

workstation

workweek

world. the world, Western world, Third World, New World, Old World. See COMPASS DIRECTIONS.

World Bank. Customary reference to the International Bank for Reconstruction and Development.

World Cup, the cup

World Series, the Series

World Wide Web, the Web. See WEB and WEB SITES.

( )worthy. Usually combines solid: airworthy.

wrack/rack. Use wrack, as a noun, to mean ruin or destruction; as a verb, use it to mean to ruin or destroy: wrack and ruin; The car was wracked up by the train. Use rack, as a noun, to mean a framework; as a verb, use it to mean to spread out, torture, trouble, torment, or score: The suspect was tortured on the rack. She racked her brain. The suspense was nerve-racking. She racked up 15 straight points.

wrangle/wangle. Wrangle means to quarrel angrily and noisily, or to herd; wangle means to bring about by persuasion or trickery.

WTO. Acceptable on second reference to World Trade Organization.

Wyoming (Wyo., WY in addresses)

Wyomingite

x. When it stands for an unknown quantity, make it italic and lowercase: *x* dollars. Capitalize references to the former film rating: a movie rated X, an X-rated movie.

X-ray

yard(s). Abbreviation, yd., acceptable only in charts, maps, and tables.

year. Abbreviation, yr., acceptable only in charts, maps, and tables. Use figures: 1964, 1964–1966, 1964–66, the 1960s, the '60s, the 1800s, mid-'90s, March 1988, the year 2000, the year 2000 problem (Y2K is acceptable when the meaning is clear). You may spell out decades when appropriate to the context: Roaring Twenties, lost in the Fifties. See AGES, DATES, and DECADES.

yellow pages. When used to mean a directory, it takes a singular verb.

yes. Capitalize if in quotes: The answer is "Yes." But The answer is yes.

yet. When it means *and* or *but,* it is a conjunction; when it means *nevertheless,* it is an adverb and should usually be followed by a comma.

young turk. Lowercase when referring to insurgents seeking to take power from an older group. Capitalize when referring to members of the early-20th-century Turkish revolutionary group.

Your Honor, etc. Capitalize Your Majesty, Her Majesty, Your Grace, Your Excellency, Your Honor, Her Royal Highness, His Eminence, etc. Lowercase my lord. Use them all only when quoting someone.

ZIP code. In addresses, use no comma between the state abbreviation and the ZIP code: 711 Keeley Street, Chicago, IL 60608. Five-digit ZIP codes are usually sufficient, but when writing nine-digit ZIP codes, as on the Contents page, use a hyphen: 2400 N Street NW, Washington, DC 20037-1196.

z's. As in An exhausted Winwood copped some serious z's before the CBGB gig.